Filmmaking, the Hard Way

A Cynical Case Study of the Feature Film Production of *All God's Creatures*

THE Indie Filmmaker Bible for Problem Solving at the Micro-Budget Level

By Josh Folan

Foreword by Ryan Gielen

Filmmaking, the Hard Way : A Cynical Case Study of the Feature Film Production of All God's Creatures

twitter.com/joshfolan

facebook.com/joshfolannyeh

joshfolan.com

twitter.com/nyehentertains

facebook.com/nyehentertainment

nyehentertainment.com

Sales Contact:

filmmakingthehardway@nyehentertainment.com

All God's Creatures stills, art and script appear courtesy of All Gods Creatures LLC.

Cover art photo credit: John Rockwell Harris

Thanks

This is a book about the making of a film, so the learning experiences I'm hoping to convey here would not exist without the contributions, and the faith in our abilities, from everyone we tried to convey our eternal gratitude to in the *All God's Creatures* credits – as well as those we regretfully forgot amidst all the chaos that is low-budget film production. Whether you are mentioned in that list or not, if you've interacted with me at any point in my tenure in this business you have a lent a hand in teaching me what I'm hoping to teach others here, and I thank you for that. So, yeah...thanks.

Phyll & Teddis – thank you for being so supportive of your needy nephew for the last twenty-plus years, and shit.

JAB – thanks for being JAB, and sorry about the drool-on-the-forehead shit.

Ryan – thanks for inspiring me to do this shit.

Meredith – thanks for reading all the shit I clutter your inbox with.

Getting Around This Book

Foreword

If you're reading this, you're probably either a filmmaker or an aspiring filmmaker, or a writer with a script that you're tired of shopping around, or a producer who wants to learn as much as possible from other people's experiences in independent film before embarking on your own indie.

You came to the right place.

You may not know me, or Josh Folan, the author, but we're part of an ever-growing group of filmmakers who have decided to take our careers and our art into our own hands. We're independent producers who just can't wait for permission to make our feature films.

The number of independent producers who are actually finishing and releasing films grows every year, and as the technology improves, the numbers will explode. This brings good news and bad news.

The bad news: Finishing an indie film will become less and less remarkable.

The good news: distributing a film, getting it seen, sold, reviewed and shared will become more and more remarkable.

This is a critical distinction.

We all share aspirations of creative freedom, and possibly even aspirations of studio success. I'm willing to bet the thing we all want most is the ability to make another film, ideally on someone else's dime. The only way this happens is if your current film is successful.

Let me restate that another way: the single most important thing you can do to become and stay a filmmaker isn't finishing your film, it's distributing your film, owning the process of audience-building, hustling every audience member you can get and making sure your baby doesn't end up collecting dust on a shelf.

Of course, recouping yours and others' investments is critical, but it's NOT the sole definition of success when starting out. It can't be. There are a dozen other measures of success when making your early films, including the opportunities it creates for you and your team. Those opportunities don't arise if you stop working after picture lock.

So what am I getting at?

I've made and released three features to date. Each one has reached a bigger platform and bigger audience than the last. Each one has higher production value, more mature storytelling, artistry and performances than the last. I love each like a child, but I have grown as have my collaborators.

One of the biggest keys to my growth, especially when distributing that first feature, has been the free sharing of ideas and best practices within the indie community. I've relied on and benefited from the experience and generous wisdom of both legendary indies like Kevin Smith and Steven Soderbergh, and less known modern indies like Arin Crumley and Susan Buice, and Lance Weiler. Legendary indie producers like Ted Hope and Christine Vachon continue to share their genius openly. Filmmaker magazine and NoFlmSchool.com take different but equally valuable approaches to helping the community learn and grow.

I've learned from their successes and mistakes, and had plenty of my own, and I feel a responsibility to share those, and I'm inspired deeply by other indies who feel the same responsibility.

Josh Folan is one of those indies. He and his small team took a tiny budget and a script they loved, with no "name" actors, they worked their tails off, sold the film to various distribution companies and recouped their investments.

They did it. They won.

Josh has spent months processing and organizing everything he learned along the way and turned it into a book that can help you do the same. This is EXACTLY what indie filmmaking is all about.

You would be hard-pressed to find another book as detailed and direct about the costs associated with getting this process right, the pitfalls, the tiny windows of opportunity that you must recognize and act upon immediately...

Filmmaking, the Hard Way isn't a be-all-end-all, it should be not the last stop on your journey, but it is a sharp, clear and incredibly helpful piece of the puzzle.

I hope you find as much inspiration and useful information as I did.

Best of luck to you on your projects,

Ryan Gielen

CUT TO:

FADE IN:

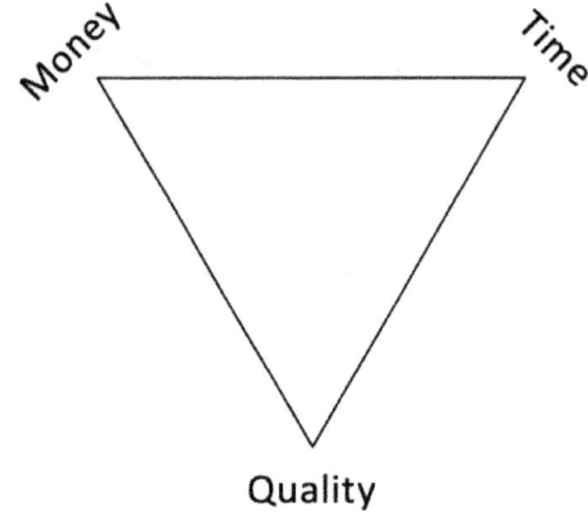

Money-Time-Quality Paradigm

Occasionally, when meandering around New York with time to kill, I'll wander into one of the few remaining capitalistic literary temples, commonly referred to by the elderly and otherwise archaically-minded as "Barnes & Noble stores." I almost never actually buy a tangible book while there; who would want those cumbersome things cluttering up their janitor's closet-sized New York apartment? Instead, I use their inventory as a means of analog googling – I root around through their shelves for film industry-related titles I have never read, and add anything of interest I find to the list in the open-ended task I always have going in my phone/Outlook for eBook download at a later time. Nine times out of ten, I find nothing of merit I haven't already digested. I have many film industry-centered sicknesses, and reading every single book pertaining to it is a close second to my cinephilesque consumption of the films themselves. So, it's safe to say I've digested enough how-to books (see my recommended reading list in the appendix) to make the generalization that even the best have a vague air about them – covering the broad strokes of making a film, but often leaving the reader wishing the magnification had been cranked up on the microscope a bit. Because of that belief, I decided to sketch this out with the intention of highlighting the specifics of the process – they won't be your specifics, as every film has its own set of challenges, but I'm hoping that our specifics will at least give you starting points for navigating through and around yours.

So again, this is not a blueprint for how to make your movie – this is a case study of how we made ours. It is not a list of solutions for the endless myriad of problems you will encounter while making the movie this hopefully helps to inspire you to create – it is a recollection of the setups and pitfalls we experienced while making *All God's Creatures* (www.allgodscreaturesfilm.com). While there could very well be an answer to a specific problem you would otherwise spend more time than you'd prefer banging your head against a wall about, the higher purpose of this writing is to demonstrate the mindset required to have even the slimmest of chances of successfully shooting, editing, and distributing a film at the micro-budget level. I've since went through the process all over again with my second feature, *What Would Bear Do?* (www.whatwouldbeardofilm.com), and I'll be sure not to shortchange you on the further teachings I've gleaned from going through the process again when they inform the steps of AGC covered in this text. Furthermore, this book is written with the assumption that the reader has some video production experience, and thereby some familiarity with the filmmaking lexicon. If you are an absolute neophyte, you shouldn't be looking to get your feet wet on a feature-length project anyhow.

The skill set that I feel is necessary to organize and execute a film production is an eclectic one, but most significant of those qualities is leadership. Regardless of your official title on the project, be it director, producer, writer, or a hybrid thereof, you are essentially running a startup business – you're the CEO. Moreover, you're running what a responsible business analyst would likely consider one of the worst kinds of business models possible. You don't have enough money to comfortably execute what amounts to your "business strategy" (making the film). There is no sign of revenue (you need a finished film to monetize before that possibility arises) on the horizon, if ever. The financial incentives a manager would optimize productivity from employees with simply do not exist – in fact you likely will need to overcome the unrest and dissent that underpaying (or not being able to pay at all) your employees creates. Most all your resources will come by way of favors (locations, equipment, labor), so you will have to find a way to facilitate their implementation at the owner's convenience, as opposed to that of the film production. The only way to overcome all this and keep the ship heading in the right direction is leadership – you will have to convincingly assure everyone inside and out that it behooves THEM for this film to reach the finish line, despite the fact they have little to no vested interest in its doing so. I hope you like to talk, and are able to do so in a tenaciously convincing fashion.

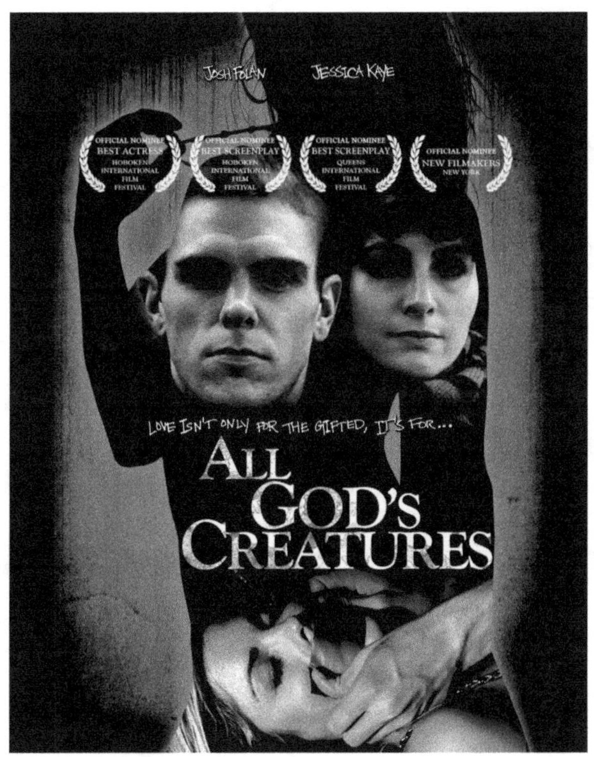

All God's Creatures One Sheet

The eternal film festival Q&A panel question, just so we have it out of the way: "how much was the budget?" Our production budget on *All God's Creatures* was $21,000, we raised another $5,000 for finishing funds in post via an Indiegogo campaign, and the four main filmmakers on the project (co-producer Matt Jared, co-directors Ryan Charles and Frank Licata, and myself) ponied up another $3700 between us to cover the cost of deliverables until the full advance was paid out by our distributor. That all translates to our "budget" being just a smidge under $30,000 USD. We played some festivals in and around New York, were nominated for some relatively meaningless – but gratifying nonetheless – awards, have received a number of reviews we are quite pleased with, and you can currently purchase the DVD from the biggest retailer in the known universe, Walmart. I believe we achieved, probably even exceeded, the blurry goals we set out to accomplish when we first met and decided to make the film in November of 2009. This is how we did it – as best as I could piece it together, anyhow.

CUT TO:

Development

Development Checklist

:: **Script, script, script.** This would seemingly be an obvious thing, yet is often overlooked. You need to have a great script. Reiteration: you need a ***great*** script. Without a great script, your chances of achieving any of your goals at the micro-budget level are null.

:: **Budget.** At the bare minimum, you need to responsibly budget the script through the end of production. Ideally, you include some money for post production and distribution costs.

:: **Business plan.** You are starting a new business with each and every film you make. Treat it accordingly and write a business plan. Even your mom won't give you money if you can't take the time to research and demonstrate a strategy for earning it back with a little ROI – or shouldn't, anyhow.

:: **Establish the company.** You need to establish a film-specific company that "owns" all the assets (and liabilities!) of the film itself.

:: **Financing.** Scratch together that sum of money however you have to go about it.

:: **Define the roles of the principal filmmakers.** At the micro-budget level, everyone is going to wear multiple hats. You need to clearly delineate what those will be before the shit hits the fan so there is accountability.

:: **Define your target and niche markets.** Know who you're making the film for and what they want to see before you make it. That way, whenever there is a question about a direction to take the film artistically (which has a tendency to get muddled amongst the chaos of production), you always have a practical, business-oriented solution to fall back on.

:: **Indie Development Legal Checklist.** Whether you're fortunate enough to have a legal professional putting them together or cautiously sorting through it yourself, these are the documents/clearances you need to have fully executed before moving on to the next phase of production – both to cover your ass, as well as to meet the delivery needs of the distributor you'll never be able to secure a deal from down the line.

:: **Fall in love with the project.** It is going to consume years of your life. If you don't believe in and love it, you'll be in for a miserable ride.

:: Script, Script, Script

Hollywood producers, or even indie producers with a few films under their belt, find their material in a number of forms – optioning novels and real life stories, purchasing spec scripts and pitches from professional writers – that require money. If you're reading this, I'm going to assume money is something you don't have. This constraint in all likelihood eliminates the above options, though I wouldn't discourage you from pursuing material you would like to develop that you view as being "out of reach." You simply never know, and it never hurts to ask. Maybe you'll be able to strike a chord with the owner of the material, and convince him you're the ideal filmmaker to communicate their story in a visual medium. This book is all about accomplishing the seemingly impossible, so pursue anything you have a passion for.

All that said, the source material for your film will likely need be born from your own imagination. If you like to write, write. If you don't like to write, find a student or aspiring screenwriter whom you share sensibilities with and help shape a screenplay with them. Just be sure to clearly define the budgetary constraints, as well as any other specifics (locations, set pieces, etc.) you might have at your disposal, to the writer in advance – you don't want the first draft showing up with a budget-gobbling opening scene set at Madison Square Garden during the halftime show of a sold-out Knicks game.

I began writing the script that would become *All God's Creatures* in June of 2008 under the working title *Untitled Love Thriller*. I, for some oddball reason, was keeping a journal about its development at the time (a practice I have never done otherwise) that lasted for a whopping five whole entries over the course of that month. According to that "journal," I beat-sheeted out the original concept - an everyman who moonlights as a serial killer – on June 10th of that year.

Poor Man's Film School Sidebar: If you don't know what a beat sheet is, you have not read Blake Snyder's bible on screenplay structure, *Save the Cat*. If that is the case, you need to delete whatever screenwriting software you have on your hard drive (Celtx is the free program I recommend) immediately and get your hands on a copy of the book. It is the be all and end all when it comes to the nuts and bolts of writing a screenplay, and to not take the time to understand the industry expectations of genre and structure before setting out to ask it for help telling your story to the world is sheer disrespect. I'd also recommend reading as many actual screenplays as you can stomach (www.imsdb.com is a gold mine) before trying to write your own. Don't just read the scripts for films you love, read some from films you loathe – it will be much easier to keep your script from sucking if you know what suck looks like.

Being my first crack at a feature-length script, it took me about a year to massage the script into a place where I felt comfortable showing it around. My producing partner at the time, Matt Jared, had a similarly-themed script he was developing, and we decided that trying to find the money to make one or the other would be easier if we shopped them around together. We quickly learned that two projects, from first time writers and being shopped by producers with no established feature production history, were every bit as difficult to find financing for as one.

While toiling away in restaurants and bars we couldn't afford to be in with supposed prospective financiers, we also were producing less daunting projects with a small, but resourceful, production team that was working under the banner of Nitty Gritty Studios (composed of director/cinematographer Frank Licata and director/editor Ryan Charles). Teamed with Nitty, we produced a slew of short form content throughout 2009, most notably a half-hour sitcom pilot entitled *Bad Apples* (www.facebook.com/badapplestv) that ended up being edited into a web series after unsuccessfully shopping it around to a few cable networks we had inlets to. We didn't necessarily realize it at the time, but we were using these projects as a means of practice for shooting a feature, which is a testament to the importance of surrounding yourself with talented and ambitious people who share your interests in filmmaking.

Without those practice swings, I doubt the four of us would have ever had the bravado to get together in my apartment in November of 2009 and decide on a start date for *All God's Creatures* of February 14th, 2010. I can't say enough about the motivational benefit of having that set time constraint. It made it real for us, and in turn prioritized our responsibilities in a way that an open-ended timetable philosophy would never have led to.

:: Budget & Business

We budgeted the script we had the best we knew how, which came to the terrifyingly miniscule figure of $19,089. There was no provision for post, contingency, or marketing costs, a mistake that would lead to countless headaches and tumultuous learning experiences down the road.

We formed a film-specific business entity that would own the film's assets, and probably more importantly, given all the chances you take with micro-budget filmmaking, its liabilities. To cover my own ass here I must recommend that you consult a legal professional for advice on how to structure your business to best suit your individual needs, but it will likely be a Limited Liability Corporation (LLC) that would be recommended to you.

Poor Man's Film School Sidebar: Most states have a website that facilitates online filing of the articles of incorporation, or similar document, which legally cements the formation of your film-specific business entity. There are quite a few companies out there that offer to perform these "legal services" for hundreds, and sometimes thousands, of dollars more than it would cost for even the most simple-minded individual to accomplish the same task in a matter of minutes. This is not intended as legal advice, but in New York State I can manage my own LLC formation and have it fully executed within twenty-four hours for $225 (the state-mandated filing fee) at the time of this writing. Most adolescent chimp amputees could accomplish the chore as well, given its ease, so you probably can too.

Poor Man's Film School Sidebar: This only works for projects that require the most minimalistic number of cast and crew, but in organizing the LLC for *What Would Bear Do?*, I offered a reasonably substantial equity stake in the company to all nine major participants in the project. Without this creative remuneration arrangement, I'd never have been able to get the required commitment out of the talented cast and crew I worked with, given how little cash was available in the budget. Don't let your creativity stop with the film itself – get creative with the business aspects too. Producing is about getting it done however you can, so figure it out.

Once you have established the company that will be accepting the limited investment dollars you will have at your production spending disposal, you will need to write a brilliant business plan. You will not be able to afford to pay someone to do this for you, so one of the principal filmmakers on your team had better have some business acumen in their repertoire to help tailor your plan in a manner that will effectively translate your creative aspirations to potential investors with no filmmaking background in a way they can understand – which hopefully will be hard numbers demonstrating the capacity for return on their investment. You can pull up the bullet point skeleton for the plan we used for *All God's Creatures* in the appendix. I didn't include the meat of the document because you should be writing the content from scratch, tailoring it to your project – not just find/replacing our title with yours and emailing it around expecting to begin collecting checks.

The cover of your plan should be your preliminary key art image – the 27x39-inch "one sheet" – that is essentially a movie poster. You don't have the luxury of production stills for this to be created from, so you'll need to find a way to convey the feel and tone of the film you intend to create without that – illustration, stock imagery, or your better idea. This will have a number of uses through production, but its utility here will be to attempt to convey the idea that the potential investor you hand and/or email the plan to is looking at an "actual movie," and the tangible thing that people equate to finished films are that staple box art/movie poster image – something you want said investor thinking about the image they are looking at on the cover of your plan when they first lay eyes on it.

Once the business plan is all ready to go, it's time to start begging for enough to cover your shoestring budget. In my experience, there are four reasons someone is willing to put money into a film:

:: **Return on investment.** With most investment ventures, this would be the sole item of importance. Given the dismal statistics on independent film ROI, there are luckily other attractors that lure money into production coffers.

:: **Film is more exciting than ball bearings.** Given the mundane makeup of most business ventures, film investment offers the financier the opportunity to rub shoulders with the entertainment community and the interesting artistic types that populate it. My own professional life having originated in finance, I can attest to this with confidence.

:: **Supporting the arts.** Some deep-pocketed individuals just want an outlet of supporting the arts that they believe in the cause of. Pitch your project right, and you could be that cause.

:: **They believe in you.** People who genuinely care about and believe in you, regardless of what it is you're doing, are likely willing to contribute to your pursuits without needing an additional incentive. Yes, this is where friends and family fall – and likely where you'll find most of the money for a first feature.

Identify what kind of investor you're dealing with before you pitch them, and tailor the pitch accordingly.

If you're lucky enough to know some people with the kind of wealth necessary to qualify as a viable film investor, you should start there and work your way down the ladder of your rolodex. Maybe prioritize the targets by the number of WaveRunners they own, most to least. With no established production history or bankable talent, you will likely find that while a lot of people love to sit down, escape their family for the evening and talk with you about making movies, very few are willing to pull the trigger and actually write a check. After enduring the song and dance of a lot of those dead ends, the final sum we were able to raise with our pretty PDF (business plan) was $20,500, the sources of which broke down as follows:

:: Matt's Parent: $6250

:: Matt's Uncle: $5000

:: My Girlfriend: $5000

:: My Aunt: $500

:: My Aunt's Parents: $850

:: A Close Friend: $500

:: Me: $2000

And that's how you finance a movie when you have no way of demonstrating to potential financiers that you're not going to basically flush their investment down the toilet. You'll notice those sources are all pretty close to home; while friends and family make a lot of sense because they believe in you, YOU MUST MAKE IT CLEAR TO THEM THAT IT IS **VERY** POSSIBLE THEY'LL NEVER SEE THAT MONEY BACK. An accredited investor accustomed to the risks of investing in film will not be happy if you flush their money down the toilet, but if you do the same with the few thousand bucks your uncle reluctantly spared from his savings without making it clear that was a distinct possibility, your family holiday gatherings are going to royally suck for quite some time.

As for the structure of the business, the four key filmmakers each owned one fourth of 51% of the entire LLC, the investors entitled to an appropriate slice (their investment / the full $20,500 sum) of the remaining 49%. There was a stipulation that the investors would be paid back the balance of their investment plus an additional ten percent before profits would be distributed across that 51/49 split, as a token of appreciation for their believing in us despite having any prudent reason for doing so. We also granted executive and associate producer credits to them.

> **Poor Man's Film School Sidebar:** It is extremely unlikely that you will find "enough" money to shoot your film. Scratch together what you can and back your budget into that amount,

and figure out a way to make it work. We spent quite a while chasing more money than we actually needed to shoot the film because we wanted to "do it right." You'll never get as much as you'd prefer, so make your movie at whatever budget level you have to and don't worry about not being able to do your script the supposed justice you feel it deserves. If the script you're developing right now is the greatest idea you'll ever have, then making films isn't what you should be doing with your time to begin with – so show the world what you can do and maybe you'll warrant a few more bucks for your next idea.

:: Define the Roles of the Principal Filmmakers

Next up was dividing key responsibilities. Ryan would be the director in charge of handling the actors on set and edit the film, Frank would be the DP/camera operator and handle most of the technical directorial duties. Matt would have a slew of customary producer responsibilities, as well as act as an AD/UPM/PA hybrid on set. I would continue to develop the script, work with Matt on all pre-production producing responsibilities, and play the lead acting role in the film. Or at least that's what we thought – undertaking something like this, with so little financial backing, inevitably results in the business owners wearing more hats than they could ever have dreamt of leading up it. We did just that.

:: Define Your Target & Niche Markets

As for defining what our audience would be, we had the luxury of subject matter featuring some very commercial elements – violence and sex. The beauty of the script itself was that while we could pitch it on the highly commercial premise that it "boiled down to a dark love story between a serial killer and a prostitute," we also knew that we were making a film that was a love story that just so happened to take place in that twisted world. We intended to walk the fine line between trying not to make it about the killing and the prostitution, but rather this off-kilter love story between two exceptionally damaged people. With those intentions, we decided that we were going after the coveted young male demographic with those more commercial elements, while keeping the love story plotline substantial enough to hopefully appeal to the headier indie/art house crowd.

In the case of niche markets, you're looking for demographics that tie into specific areas of your subject matter in some way. Jon Reiss' books, particularly *Think Outside the Box Office*, deal heavily in helping you identify and target your potential niches, and I highly recommend you get your hands on and consume these before moving past this step in the process. In a nutshell, you want to find things in your script's content that are very specific, and then figure out what kind of person would be interested in that particular type of subject matter. If you have positive religious undertones in your story, you should certainly think about what kind of religious groups and associated organizations you could market the film to. With AGC we had serial killer themes (the appropriate subject matter to immediately segue to after using religion as an example, obviously) and there are a shocking number of blogs and special interest groups out on the interwebs that deal in that stuff, so one of our many plans was to locate and pursue some placement in that community once we were in a position to monetize any possible interest that was driven up.

:: Indie Development Legal Checklist

:: Articles of Organization for your film-specific company. The filing with the state that legitimizes the existence of said company.

:: Operating Agreement (LLC)/Corporate By-Laws (Standard Corporation)/Partnership Agreement (LLP). These are all different names for the detailed internal document that explains how your company will be managed and within what parameters it will do business.

:: Screenplay chain of title. If the screenplay is an original work, this would be made up of the document filing receipt from the U.S. Copyright Office and a literary acquisition agreement between the writer and the film company. It could also include clearances from the person or estate of the person a biopic focuses on, clearances from the author of an original work in the case of the screenplay being based on a novel, etc. – ultimately it's the shit that says you own the story told in your movie.

:: Apply for federal tax ID number, open an operating account at a bank, get each financial controller – likely the producers and eventually a UPM, if you are fortunate enough for those to not be the same person...that person being you – a debit/credit card. You need somewhere to stash all the money you're not going to be able to raise to shoot the film.

:: Crew deal memos for the core filmmakers. Just because you're the figureheads of the operation does not mean there shouldn't be a document clearly defining each of your roles and responsibilities with the company. The individuals who are financially responsible for the budget should be specified here, as well as who will have final say in creative issues (particularly final cut) and/or how those creative differences will be resolved in the event of a disagreement. We chose a majority vote of the four main filmmakers as our system, not the wisest verdict seeing as that's an even number that could have resulted in a troublesome stalemate – something we somehow never encountered.

:: Fall In Love with the Project

What kinds of films do you like to watch? What are the films that, when channel surfing, you will stop on every single time you see them, regardless of where in the runtime it happens to be? Whatever those films are, you will need to love your baby at least as much. It's not unrealistic to say you will watch it hundreds of times in varying degrees of completion over the next one to four years, so it better be about something you like a whole hell of a lot. If it doesn't excite you to read the script at square one, find another script – if you don't, you'll loathe the seventh (and still "rough") cut with a passion you didn't know you could muster.

CUT TO:

Pre-Production

Pre-Pro Checklist

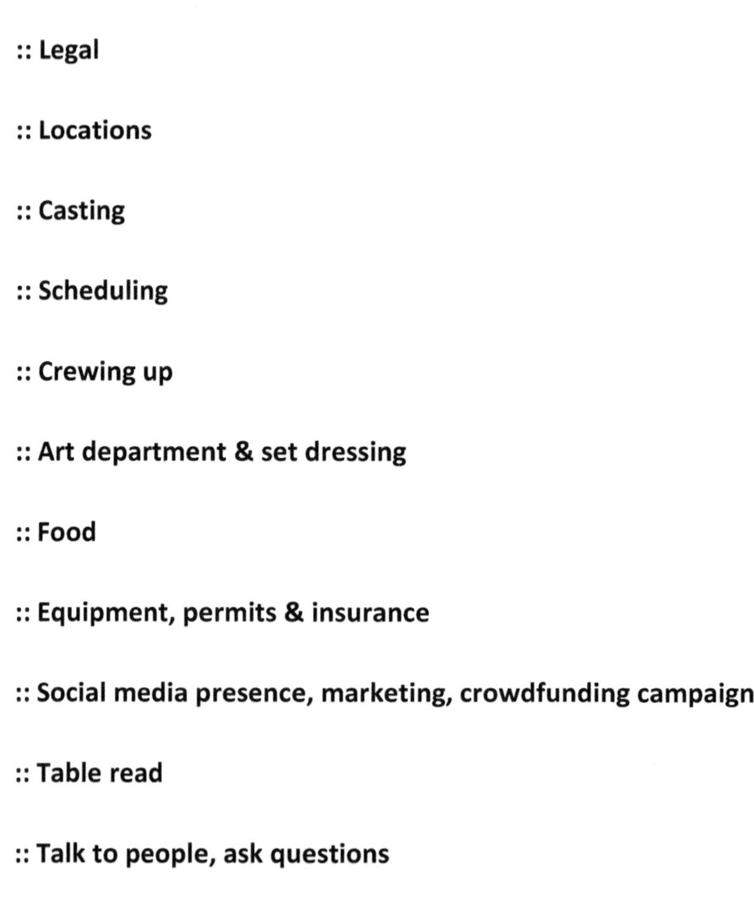

:: Legal

:: Locations

:: Casting

:: Scheduling

:: Crewing up

:: Art department & set dressing

:: Food

:: Equipment, permits & insurance

:: Social media presence, marketing, crowdfunding campaign

:: Table read

:: Talk to people, ask questions

:: Indie Pre-Pro Legal Checklist

:: Are you ready?

We set a pre-production start date of the first Monday of the year, January 4th, 2010. You may or may not have noticed there was no mention of finishing up and locking the script in the development phase. This is a heinous, blood-curdling mistake – one I have not made since or will ever make again. We chose to make that mistake as part of the "just do it" mentality that we adopted in my apartment in that first meeting, thinking we could just fix it as we went along. It would be a difficult thing to overcome in a properly-funded production setting, seeing as every single aspect of your production planning is based on that script, so having that in flux while trying to secure locations, cast members and other critical elements makes it exponentially more difficult than it would be otherwise. In our entirely-devoid-of-funding setting it really dialed up the nut-squeeze of us not having enough money. If there's one thing you take from this text, take this: finish your goddamn script before starting to schedule and plan production from it.

While we didn't know how big a mistake it was to start pre-pro without the script finished, we did have a vague understanding that it was bad, so one of our first action items was rectifying that issue. Ryan had a good friend that is a hell of a playwright, so we collectively decided to have him do a pass on it to tie up some of the loose ends I was having trouble with. An area he really helped with was punching up the female characters, which is one of the areas of my writing I still tend to have trouble with. Being my first feature and swamped with producing responsibilities those characters without question benefited from his work on the script, particularly the lead character of Delia. His contributions would continue up through the first couple days of shooting.

:: Legal

If you don't have inexpensive/free legal counsel at your disposal, you will need to find a way to navigate all the legal paperwork required to safely ensure everyone and everything will be in place when the little red button gets pressed for the first time on day one of shooting. Before anyone will give you a dime for your work, you will need chain of title documents, location agreements, cast and crew deal memos, music licensing agreements and an assortment of other clearances. At the very least, you will be relying on that really business-savvy member of your core team to find pro-forma documents that you can tweak to fit your production's needs.

> **Poor Man's Film School Sidebar:** We were able to barter for some legal advice by offering a role to an actor who happened to also be a lawyer. #problemsolver

Mark Litwak is a well-traveled entertainment attorney who has published a number of books wherein standard contracts to work from lie, and you can also find a number of documents at filmmakeriq.com/2009/04/588-free-film-contracts-and-forms/. You can fill these needs without spending thousands and thousands of dollars to have a lawyer draft all-too-similar documents from supposed scratch, but it is highly recommended you find a way to get approval on the end product from a law professional before moving forward in the process.

While using union crew is pretty much out of the question at the micro-budget level, you do have a decision to make when it comes to hiring union actors. SAG-AFTRA has a number of low-budget agreements and can be very accommodating in working with producers on smaller films, but they can also be quite rigid when they think union members might be at risk of being shortchanged or mistreated by awarding your project union status. We chose to go non-union with *All God's Creatures*, and it worked for us and allowed us to get away with some scheduling expectations from our cast we probably would not have been able to afford if we'd have been a union production, and that allowed us to save a few bucks we could spend on other areas. What's right for you will depend on your casting needs and decisions.

:: Locations

On a $20k production budget, renting sound stages and building sets from scratch is out of the question – which forces you into a location-shooting-only scenario where you'll be exposed to all sorts of environmental risks and inconveniences that make everything more difficult than they would be in an in-studio setting. It also means you'll have to find and scout the locations, figure out a way to get access to the owner/decision maker, and then beg them to allow you to shoot there at a time that doesn't decimate your production schedule for little or no money. If you can't afford a location manager and/or scouts, guess who's going to be doing all that legwork...

One upside to this can be the authenticity and production value that can be gleaned from shooting in well-chosen locations, value that can extend well beyond that with which your financial means should allot you access to. A great deal of money is often spent decorating sets to make them look "lived in," but a good (or lucky) scouting eye can find that genuine feel at little or no cost out in the real world. We had a few instances where our financial constraints forced us into shooting in places that ultimately lent themselves to the gritty tone of the film, whereas our first options would likely have been much too glossy for what ended up being appropriate.

All God's Creatures had about 20 first unit locations and a few smaller ancillary b-roll setups. Some of our needs were terribly demanding given our meager location fee budget; a railroad yard, a coffee shop, a fast food restaurant, an office setting, a river, a suburban household. We also needed a couple NYC apartments for the two lead characters. How we found and secured each:

:: **Apartments.** We were looking at about five days, almost a third of the schedule, spread across the two lead character's apartments. The bulk of our shooting was sizing up to be in Manhattan, which is where both Matt and I's apartments were located and they worked aesthetically, so it was pretty much a given from the start we would be inviting a movie crew in to trash our pads for the shoot. Matt's apartment also doubled as the production office – wardrobe, craft services, equipment and any other production need that required a staging point had a home there.

:: **Employee Break Room.** This was a tough one. The idea was for it to look like whatever an AMTRAK employee break room might look like, which we originally assumed any traditional office break room with a water cooler and a coffee pot would suffice for. If you have money to pay for it, these are pretty abundant. We did not, which relegated us to asking friends with office jobs if we could intrude on their place of employment for a night in exchange for...nothing. Except for a special thanks credit which, on a little film like ours, is the equivalent of shit stuck to your shoe. We didn't have any takers on that attractive proposition, surprisingly, and eventually came up with the alternative idea of a locker room. Matt happened to belong to a 24-hour gym in West Harlem near his apartment on 148th Street, where he hunted down the manager and convinced him to let us come in with a skeleton crew at midnight and shoot the scene. I believe we paid something like $100 to cover some sort of administration cost on their end in exchange, in addition to agreeing to apply some shit to the manager's shoe.

:: **Claw Machine Game.** Originally slated for the lobby of a movie theater, we quickly realized (even with the help of some film commissions) that we were not going to be able to secure a movie theater lobby of any kind on the cheap, let alone one that happened to have a claw machine. I received constant pressure to cut this from the script because of these difficulties, but I was pretty hard-headed about it and insisted I would find a solution. I lived on East 108th Street at the time, and there was a deli on the corner of that and 2nd Avenue that I passed by every day walking to the subway. The deli happened to have a decrepit claw machine game sitting out front on the sidewalk, and once we came to the conclusion a movie theater was not going to happen I started stopping in every afternoon, asking to speak to the owner/manager and leaving a business card, for weeks until I had gotten a signature on a location agreement to shoot there. What seemed like a concession at the time actually turned out to be a positive, as the rough Spanish Harlem exterior was far more appropriate for the film than a brightly-lit theater lobby.

:: **Coffee Shop.** The main character was written as working at a mom-and-pop coffee house, and we were looking at a solid two days of interior shooting at the location. There was no way to creatively work around the need for an actual coffee shop, and small coffee shops don't have much of an online presence, so we set out to find it the old fashioned way: on-foot location scouting. For a few weeks in a row, we got up early on a Saturday and stomped the streets of Manhattan's Lower East Side trying to find a café that would be open to our intrusion and faux-budget. Eventually we located a place on one of the avenues too cool and/or far East to be numbered, negotiated an hourly rate and schedule that seemed like it would work, and signed the paperwork. As often happens in micro-budget filmmaking, chaos ensued the day before we started filming when the manager called to inform us that we would not be able to shoot at his establishment for reasons I can't recall. In a fit of producing wizardry, Matt began googling his way down Broadway from 148th Street, hitting up every single coffee shop along the way until he found a store owner that loved movies enough to let us shoot ours in his place for, I believe, something like $250/night and buying our meals from their food menu.

:: **Dive Bar.** I bartended at a place in Murray Hill and the manager was an investor, making this one pretty easy. We'd load in at 3 AM leading up the bar closing at 4 AM and shoot overnight. Because of our confidence in the location, we scheduled it for the first day of shooting.

:: **Employment Agency Office.** Another office location, this one without the complication of needing a break room – all we needed was a desk in a typical office setting. A friend of Matt's offered his up until the morning of the night we were scheduled to shoot there, when I woke up to a voicemail from him informing me that was no longer the case. Chaos again overtook until I was able to get a hold of the owner of the office Matt worked in, which was the preexisting backup plan. Easier said than done, but always have a backup plan.

:: **Hotel Lobby & Room.** Another one that was relatively easy. Seedy was the desired motif, so we shopped around at exquisite by-the-hour motels in the neighborhood near the Harlem production office and found a place that would let us get some quick lobby and hallway shots as long as we rented a room for the duration of the time we were shooting there. Some of the best production value "bang for our buck" we got out of the entire shoot.

:: **Subway/Train.** You can't afford to get this "legitimately" at this level, so if you need footage on a moving train you'll have to keep it simple and sans sound capture, have a lightweight camera and your actors in costume and ready to go, and renegade it.

:: **Movie Theater.** Matt had a friend that managed The Abingdon Theatre on 36th Street, so we were able to get a couple of hours there one morning for a nominal fee.

:: **Restaurant.** Yet another walk-into-every-single-option-around-the-production-office-until-we-got-lucky situation. We found a beautiful place only a few blocks away, which looks really great in the footage that we eventually let fall to the cutting room floor. You do a lot of thankless work in film production.

:: **Taco Hut.** A short prank phone call scene with the leads required showing the victim of the call on the other end of the line, which was set in the kitchen of a takeout joint. We found it by walking into places near Matt's apartment as well, and secured it in exchange for agreeing to buy dinner there the night of the shoot.

:: **Suburban House.** Two full days of shooting here, including a very touchy rape scene – as I'm sure any rape dramatization is. Ryan and Frank had an aunt on Staten Island with an ideal house that was kind enough to all but vacate and allow us free reign over.

:: **River.** The waterways in NYC are under strict regulation by the parks department and the coast guard, so while the Mayor's Office of Film was able to steer us in all the right directions, it was still quite a bit of legwork to secure the proper permits for us to be able to light (which required a generator – an equipment need that makes renegade shooting out of the question) and properly capture the night scenes we needed to shoot down in Riverbank State Park in West Harlem.

:: **Rail Yard.** With no possibility whatsoever of getting a large rail company to allow us access to a rail yard, this one required some serious research – even to the point where my co-producer was pushing me to change the location in the script to something that would be easier to procure. I turned to the film commissions, which are profoundly helpful organizations located most everywhere in the country and in quite a few places worldwide, and whose sole purpose is to help attract production to the area they preside over by way of helping to find anything and everything a producer needs to shoot there. The Association of Film Commissioners International website (www.afci.org) is where to start this process, which I did, and they eventually directed me to the Suffolk County Film Commission – which in turn put me in touch with Bill Bell, the curator of the Oyster Bay Railroad Museum, a really cool organization with a number of old locomotives and various other pieces of rail equipment in yard near the museum itself. They just happened to have had recently started entertaining the possibility of creating an income stream for the museum by offering film productions the opportunity to shoot there – AGC would be a "test run" for them, and we couldn't have been happier to be their guinea pig. Huge producer victory dance upon securing this particular location agreement.

Poor Man's Film School Sidebar: When Bill Bell read the script to ensure it was something he was comfortable with the museum associating itself with, his only feedback, other than generic positives, was that we should change the horse-hair shaving brush Jon uses in the beginning of the film to a badger-belly-hair brush. Delving deeper into his reasoning, I found that Bill considers himself somewhat of a "shaving enthusiast," and badger-belly hair is a much softer and desirable choice for a shaving brush. I didn't hesitate to make the change in the script, and immediately informed Bill that he would officially be credited in the film as a "shaving consultant." It was a cost-free, but creative, gesture that made him laugh and permanently aligned him with our interests. Sometimes that's your most influential tool as a producer – making the person you're asking help of chuckle.

Your production bible should have a worksheet for each location with owner and all on-site contact information for the days you could potentially be shooting there, approved power source locations, parking, holding, changing and bathroom facility location, as well as any other info that would be helpful to making the organization and execution of the shoot there go as smoothly as possible.

:: Casting

"I know a guy who caters with a guy who body-doubled for [insert really marketable star name here] for two days on that really [clever adjective] film that won best [academy award category] last year. We should have that guy send that other guy the script so he can give it to [aforementioned movie star]."

Guess what? That aforementioned star can't do your movie, even if they wanted to. Their world-class representatives are not going to let them forego world-class acting fees (ten percent of which goes to those reps – highly motivational for said reps) on studio-backed projects that will be seen in every multiplex on the planet, to spend eighteen sixteen-hour days running around with your inexperienced cast and crew making a movie that will (relatively speaking) be seen by no one. This selective mentality is also the basis for the market-making demand every agent hopes to curate for their clients – if they said yes to everyone, demand would go down for their services and, in turn, the fees they are able to require for their client's participation in a project. The exception to this rule is having a relationship with an A-list actor who's willing to take the risk of pissing off their agent to do you a solid and allow you to shamelessly use their name to help sell your film...and if you are that exception, why the hell are you bothering to read this book? Go exploit them and invite me to your chateau at Sundance next year.

It is far more likely you will spend a great deal of time painstakingly navigating the treacherous waters of unrepresented/undiscovered actor casting, hoping to stumble onto someone brilliant to help carry your film.

> **Poor Man's Film School Sidebar:** One no-cost thing you can do to increase your odds of finding great actors at bargain-basement pricing is to find a young intern or associate working under a reputable casting director in your market (granted, a much tougher thing to do if you're not in a major market like NY or LA) who is willing to help cast your film in exchange for their first casting director credit on a feature. They'll have access to a

number of resources (talent, facilities, etc.) that are beyond yours, be able to offer professional insight on your casting decisions, as well as lend an otherwise unachievable air of legitimacy to the project by way of their association with the casting director they work under. We were fortunate to have Sarah Tillson, who was working with Elissa Myers at the time, agree to come on board in that capacity.

The way you approach your casting will be the first statement you make to your talent about the level of professionalism they will be working in, should they be cast in your film. You will need them to be at the top of their game to keep your shoot on time and under budget, so it is critical that you project that same level of expected professionalism back at them in your casting process. I come from an acting background, and nothing cools my interest in a project more than walking into a bush-league audition setting. Some ground rules:

:: Breakdown Services (www.breakdownservices.com) **MUST** be your first avenue for putting out the casting breakdown, which should be well written and interesting. BS is the industry standard, particularly with agents and managers, for receiving these things, and anywhere else is going to be disregarded by most all professionals. The one exception to this is having an especially unique character type to cast – a Native American paraplegic who can play the harmonica well, for example. You should still start with Breakdown Services, but if that doesn't drive up any viable options it will then be time to start begin seeking out alternative means for filling the role. Craigslist is always an option, albeit an often disappointing one, and there are a million others that are just one google away.

> **Poor Man's Film School Sidebar:** Every character in your script, if it's a good script, will have something unique and or interesting built into the text; even down to the most insignificant day player role. If there is not, because the writer was too lazy to do so, take the time to jazz up their existence here. "[Old Farmer] 50's-60's, he farms" is not a character description that is going to make any worthwhile actor's ears perk up. If you were able to secure a casting director, they should be handling a lot of the heavy lifting with the character breakdowns. A breakdown from *What Would Bear Do?* that I'm happy to share:
>
> *Rachel: Early to mid-twenties. Cute exterior masking a dry, sarcastic nature with vehement capabilities when she is set off – something that doesn't take all that much to provoke. Needs to be damn funny, and great with improv.*

:: Email them one or two (a second one should be a strong contrast from the first) scenes from the script ("sides") for their character in advance so they can properly prepare the material. The audition environment is inherently awful enough, not allowing the actors to prepare their best effort because you're afraid of your "precious material" ending up on the interwebs is asinine.

:: Nudity. I recommend you try to avoid its necessity at this level of production. That said, we asked it of some of the cast members in *All God's Creatures*. If you decide it's a requisite to tell your story, you must be straightforward about that decision and state its nature and usage in a very concise manner at every step of the casting process, starting with the breakdown you send out. You're asking a lot of an actor to go that far for you, and you need to expect to work twice as hard to provide a safe and comfortable environment for them to do so in. Rehearse the scenes (fully clothed) with all actors involved in advance, provide a closed set with as few crew members present as possible, have robes at arm's length while shooting, etc. Basically, be accommodating in every way imaginable. And if it is a necessary part of playing the role, make sure you have a written agreement in place stating any and all expectations long before you are on set.

:: Get a professional space to hold the auditions in. Even if you have to pay full price for it, studio space is $12-15 an hour. It's worth it, for your convenience and the actors'.

:: Have at least a sign-in sheet in the waiting area to keep the actors organized in a clearly defined queue, if not an unpaid intern to moderate said queue.

:: Record video of the auditions for review. Have a spreadsheet prepared for everyone sitting in on the auditions to take notes about each actor on.

:: In the room etiquette: the actor comes in, hands you their picture and resume. You say hi, do your best to make small talk, ask if they have any questions about the material. Again, if you have a casting director they will alleviate most of the responsibility in this awkward exchange. You can even delegate the first round of auditions to them entirely, where they will narrow down the field to only the best candidates in their eyes and schedule a second round of auditions where you can work with and get a feel for them. After those initial pleasantries you (or the CD) should ask for a slate, then shut the fuck up and let the actor give their prepared audition. Once that is done, you are free to direct away – whether that be interrupting, giving direction, whatever – but let them give their own take on it first. You might even see something amazing you hadn't thought of, so don't squander an opportunity for free ideas with your verbose film auteur nonsense.

Poor Man's Film School Sidebar: On *What Would Bear Do?*, I took an unorthodox approach to the casting process that I highly recommend for leading roles. In casting the role of Rachel, which was ultimately portrayed brilliantly in the film by Graci Carli, it was important to me that I have an actress that could handle the small nature of the production and being on location in Cleveland, where the shooting would take place. I started the process the same way, putting out a breakdown, but instead of scheduling auditions from those submissions, I sent out sides to actresses that fit the physical type and requested an audition video be emailed in. From those I selected the handful of performances I liked the most, and **then** scheduled meetings with them – and even then these meetings were generals, a short meeting where we could just talk and get to know each other without the awkward pressure of an audition environment. The actresses that seemed a good fit for the project in that process were then called in to read on camera with the actor playing opposite them – which was me. This approach saved me a ton of time I'd have spent with actresses not right for the project if I'd have done things as they usually are, and allowed me to get a feel for the *person* I'd be going on location to work with in a low-budget filmmaking setting – an environment that is tenuous enough in the best-case scenario, and one that can become a complete nightmare if you don't like the people you're cooped up with.

:: Scheduling

On a "real movie" you would enlist the help of an experienced line producer to sort out your shooting schedule – a mind-numbing matrix of variables that are constantly in flux. Without money, one of your core team members will be the poor schmuck that endures this miserable responsibility. The equation? You take the overall shooting schedule length limitations (which you don't really have enough money to pay for food and other operating costs during), add the location (which you're not paying the owners of enough to inconvenience them and/or disrupt their business) scheduling constraints, then finally factor in the hectic scheduling demands of actors (whom you can't afford to pay "real" day rates to begin with, let alone for the consecutive employment fees necessary to warrant them blocking off the entire shooting schedule in their calendars). A + B + C = X, right? It should be simple. It is not.

There are a number of software options to make it easier, the most popular being Movie Magic Scheduling, which is offered as a bundle with their equally as popular Budgeting program for around $750. You can get away with knocking out both tasks on a single film project for free with their trial editions available for download on their website at www.entertainmentpartners.com.

Once you finally figure it all out, you'll inevitably lose a location and have to replace it with another that has polar-opposite scheduling requirements. You will adjust the schedule. Then your lead actor will email you saying they booked a ShamWow instructional video, a gig that will pay them twenty times the paltry day rate you are offering, and they need to ensure availability for the shoot dates on that or they have to bow out of the project. You will adjust the schedule. Then that actor will call you and say the shoot dates on the ShamWow job have been pushed back by a week. You will adjust the schedule again. That's all before the end of the first twenty-four hour period of having sent out the "finished" schedule. This perpetual state of insanity will occur in Groundhog Day-like repetition every day until the end of principal photography. #ohmygodkillmenow just thinking about it.

Some scheduling tips that could potentially save you some production dollars:

:: Try to schedule your exteriors towards the beginning of your shoot, so when you wake up to a torrential downpour the weather channel was unable to predict, you have interior days with flexible scheduling options at your disposal.

:: This is might be an obvious one, but try to schedule in a way that facilitates shooting out anything or anyone that weighs heavily on the production budget – locations, actors, vehicles, etc.

:: Keep exorbitant equipment needs clumped together. Night exteriors will likely need more elaborate lighting and a generator, try to shoot those scenes together so as to minimize the time you keep those costly items on hand (without the legwork of returning and reacquiring them over and over). Keep the same thing in mind for any dolly needs. The ideal scheduling conditions will likely need retooling after the shot list is finalized between your director and DP.

:: Crewing Up

One upside to no money or resources of any kind is you don't have to spend as much time as you otherwise would to acquire and organize the production elements they would allow for. This wonderful "advantage" will be particularly prevalent when you start rounding out your crew. Not only do you not have money to pay their wages, but every additional crew member is also another mouth to feed and body to transport. Because you will likely be shooting long days to make your schedule, it will be two meals that you're feeding to those additional mouths on a lot, if not all, your shooting days. Knowing this, you should make every effort you can to find people who are capable of wearing many hats. Our co-directors were also the editor and DP, and Frank was not only the DP, but also the camera operator. Three jobs, one mouth to feed - that's how you drag a micro-budget film shoot to the finish line.

> **Poor Man's Film School Sidebar:** In asking these people to help you achieve your cinematic vision for so little more than exercising their love for filmmaking, you inherently are agreeing to an unwritten rule – under absolutely no circumstance should you be making a dime more from the production than the lowest man/woman on your production totem pole. You're the owner of the material, and if the collective succeeds in making something great, all the financial and critical successes will be yours – so If you can't at the least make the same sacrifices you're asking of your cast and crew, you are an asshole.

How we crewed up:

:: **Cinematographer.** As already mentioned, one of our core filmmakers, co-director Frank Licata, was our DP and camera op. He owned a Panasonic HVX-200, saving us a boatload in camera rental costs, and did not require an AC.

:: **Editor.** The other co-director, Ryan Charles, was our editor. Having your editor on set is always an asset, as you then have a built-in manager of the digital media storage your precious footage resides on, and it allows for a more knowledgeable assembly of the rough cut as shooting progresses. This arrangement does compromise the time available for that assembly, given your director must of course focus on directing, but for a micro-budget production that is a concession you are happy to live with given the fiscal upside.

:: **Art Director.** A good friend of our co-director Frank, Jennifer Woo, handled the art direction for the film. Her background dealt heavily in theater art direction, which meant the allure of her first feature film credit (a recurring theme you must exploit at the micro-budget level) and being Frank's friend were enough to get her to sign on at no cost other than covering her expenses. She, along with production designer Victor Medina-San Andres, would go on to do an amazing job making the serial killer character's "lair" look as disturbing and twisted as it needed to.

:: **Production Designer.** A Craigslist ad put Victor in front of us, and we were able to convince him to work with Jennifer on the same basis – just covering his expenses.

:: **Make-Up Artist.** We had worked with Aubrey Neal on *Bad Apples*, and because of her "can do" attitude and willingness to do anything and everything asked of her in a filmmaking setting, we didn't hesitate to offer her the job. That's something you should look for regardless of the scale of the production, but particularly so in micro-budget settings – the willingness to do whatever needs to be done to get the shot. Your make-up artist is there for the beautification of the actors, but that doesn't mean she can't hold a bounce card so your cinematographer can get a shot when we're short on available hands – or shouldn't anyhow, though most unions would disagree. Aubrey was also willing to tackle the light make-up effects responsibilities (i.e. blood – and there's that multiple hats concept again) that the subject matter demanded.

:: **Assistant Director.** We "awarded" this all-important position to a guy that was willing to let us borrow a small lighting package we direly needed for the shoot, but just as we were rolling into production he notified us that he probably wouldn't be able to make to most of the days. He ended up making it to none, and either my co-producer Matt or myself ended up keeping us on schedule overall. Shot-to-shot time management and decisions were handled by our script supervisor, Erika Sanz, and the co-directors, which isn't something I'd recommend. Do your best to get an AD on set to keep an eye on the overall picture and make sure the day's shot list is being fully covered, and if you're forced to make cuts because of time that they are responsibly decided upon.

:: **Script Supervisor.** There will not be a single moment over the course of your shoot where you and most of your crew are not thinking about time. And money. And one or more crisis. Having someone whose sole responsibility is adhering to the text on your set is critical, and the importance of that dedicated set of eyes and ears of course only increases amidst the chaos that is micro-budget filmmaking. We were able to find Erika Sanz through craigslist at minimal cost on the condition that if she were able to find higher-paying work during the shoot we couldn't say anything about her absence.

:: **Key Grip/Set Operations Utility Infielder.** Our co-director, Ryan, had a good friend with some light production experience that was able to come down from Hartford and crash on his couch for the duration of the shoot and be our savior on many of occasions, basically in exchange for food. Matt Hennessey did everything - lighting setup, driving responsibilities, equipment load-in and out, multiple unrecognizable background player cameos, and even a small speaking role at one point. He was the crew member that micro-budget producer dreams are made of.

:: **Gaffer.** Nicalena Iovino was referred to us as a gaffer looking to build her resume, and she worked for us when other (paid) work didn't prevent her doing so in exchange for credit and a monthly MTA Metrocard. She was a total honey badger.

:: **Wardrobe Supervisor.** There wasn't anything too demanding in the wardrobe department, mostly just rifling through actor's existing wardrobe for what works with the character and keeping an eye on it once we started shooting, so we didn't have to find anyone all that seasoned here. Co-director Ryan Charles' girlfriend at the time, Veronique Hurley, is an actress so we bartered a small role in exchange for helming the department.

:: **Art Department Assistant/Prop Master.** The other co-director's girlfriend was friends with our lead art director and offered to help in these capacities.

:: **Still Photographer.** We found John Rockwell Harris through Craigslist, and he was a godsend. I still don't really know why he was willing to work on the film, given his resume at the time. I think his being from Cleveland, as I am, was probably the only reason he agreed to come to six key days of shooting on our more high production value sets. He is due photo credit for every single piece of marketing we put together for the film, and without the neatly-organized DVD set he passed off after the shoot we would have not been able to extend our marketing and distribution reach anywhere near as comprehensively as we did.

> **Poor Man's Film School Sidebar:** This is an often overlooked position at the micro-budget level, but you MUST have a photographer getting good stills during the shoot so you have something to create marketing materials from down the road. You'll never be able to afford to get the actors together, in costume with the right length/style hair, in the proper setting to shoot publicity material again, so you better have someone who knows what they're doing taking care of it while you worry about shooting your movie. An experienced production photographer will know how to get in there and get the shot before, during, and after takes without

the slightest impediment to the precious shooting schedule.

And that was our big, bad indie film crew. It may seem small, and I've since shot a feature with even less available hands, but the important thing is to responsibly calculate what it is your project needs to reach the finish line and finding the leanest way possible of fulfilling those needs. There's no blueprint for that – every project is its own unique beast, and a good producer can gauge and procure to the material's needs accordingly.

:: Art Department & Set Dressing

The budget for the art department was pretty much nil, and while we were fortunate that the story was written to keep the needs here to a minimum, there were still a few things that needed to be addressed. We were blessed to have Jennifer and Victor heading up these responsibilities, as they both had a wealth of knowledge on how to solve problems and make things happen on the cheap. The two major art needs they addressed are below, all other locations were scouted and secured with the intention of shooting them relatively as is.

:: Serial Killer's Bedroom. This set was an extreme overhaul of my actual bedroom in my apartment, which needed to be transformed from an IKEA-infused minimalistic setting into a terrifying shrine dedicated to a killer's lineage of slain young women. To up the difficulty, it would need to be built from scratch inside 48 hours in the middle of the shoot – more on that circus in the production section. The job ultimately required a repainting of the room, some furniture building, and a ton of small art projects aimed at conveying the disturbance that was the lead character's mindscape – all for about a $100 run to Home Depot. Jennifer's creativity even extended to suggesting the use of the hardcopy headshots of actresses we didn't go with in our casting process – which we would have just chucked out otherwise, after digitizing the info into our actor rolodex – as set pieces, cutting their eyes out and distressing the pictures. Brilliant stuff. The end result was every bit as jarring as we asked them to make it.

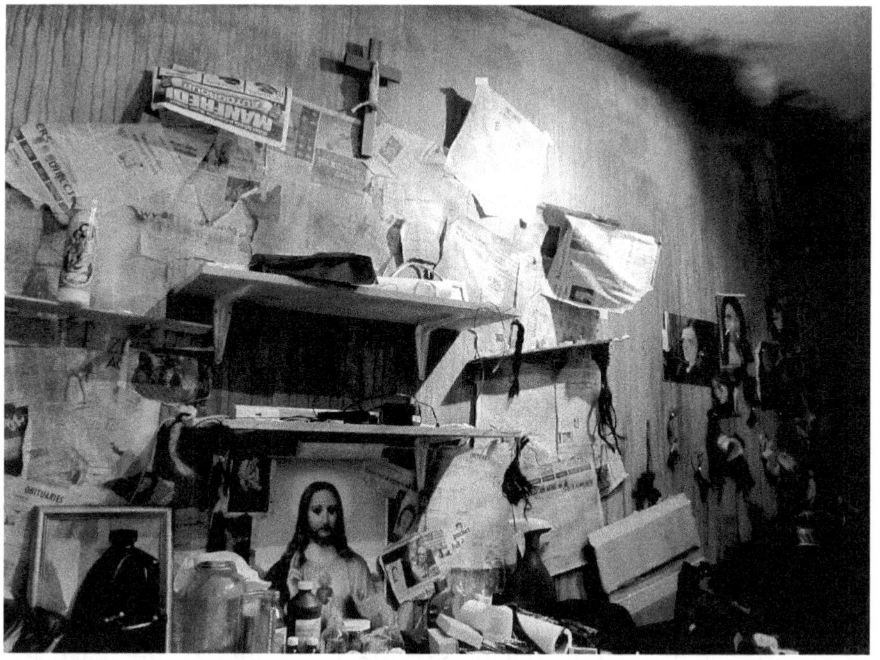

Serial Killer Bedroom Set

:: **Delia's Apartment.** We had a couple instances of fortuity in pre-production where beautiful set pieces were stumbled upon in NYC trash. I found a lamp that screamed "Delia" to me in the trash behind my building the week before the shoot, and Matt came upon an incredible pink-upholstered chair a month or so prior. Both would become focal points of this set. To fill the rest of it out, Jennifer consulted Film Biz Recycling (www.filmbizrecycling.org) in Gowanus, Brooklyn – an amazing nonprofit outfit that rents props and such that are donated by productions that would otherwise throw them away after their shoot.

:: Food

What the hell you're going to eat everyday would seemingly be one of the lesser concerns in the grand scheme of organizing a film shoot, but you will quickly see when you start asking your cast and crew about their dietary preferences and restrictions that everyone has different wants and needs you will have to accommodate. To not do so will only create dissent and diminish productivity, which will in turn hurt your bottom line – so find out, in depth, what those needs are and exceed them.

> **Poor Man's Film School Sidebar:** The easiest way to gather this data is to whip up a simple one-sheet questionnaire asking about allergies, dietary restrictions, emergency contact info, and any other wants or needs they might have, and have it filled out along with the person's contract/deal memo. It'll make you seem like a compassionate, accommodating person…even if you're really a take no prisoners, indie filmmaking slave-driver type like I am.

As for what to actually eat, you'll have to figure that out on your own. The one definitive I have for you on this is that if you try to buy Subway sandwiches every meal of every day like we did on AGC, people will begin to bitch around day four or five at the very latest.

:: Equipment, Permits & Insurance

With your crew in place and scheduling out of the way, the director and producer should sit down and put together a day-to-day shot list with the DP and get a chronologically-organized list of equipment needs together. Your DP will likely push for more than you can afford, and it will be the producer's responsibility to "talk him or her down" to what the budgetary constraints allow for. Once you have your equipment list down to what your budget will allow, check those needs with any grip or electric department crew members to see if they have any of it available for rental from their personal kits before approaching rental houses for quotes – they likely will be willing to provide what they have at a far better rate. Don't be shy about comparison shopping with rental houses, and don't hesitate to tell a rep a hard price you're willing to pay for the package you need. If your rental period falls into a slow period for the house, they will be happy to generate below-expectation rental income instead of having that stuff sit on shelves in their warehouse. Everything is negotiable. The same goes for vehicle needs. See if you can get away with just a fifteen-passenger van before getting a box truck for equipment as well. Parking is costly and extra aggravation if you're in a large metropolis, not to mention the rental and fuel costs of the truck itself.

Most cities have a department that handles the issuance of film production permits, and some light googling should lead you to the appropriate contact for any municipalities you intend to shoot in. All but one of our locations fell under the jurisdiction of the New York Mayor's Office of Film, Theatre & Broadcasting, which was a blessing to work with. It was a no-cost endeavor that simply required filling out some paperwork and showing proof of insurance, though they've since instituted a $300 application fee. Our one location outside of their authority was in Oyster Bay out on Long Island, where the railroad museum we were shooting the film's climax at was located. That permit ran us $500, which we all found pretty ironic – a tiny town on long island required such a large fee, while shooting in the most densly-populated city in the country was free.

Production insurance is a costly but necessary evil if you are using union actors, renting equipment or any vehicles, or applying for shooting permits. Even if none of the above apply, it's still a wise investment in case anything should happen to go wrong on set. Owing a location a bunch of money because something was accidentally knocked over while everyone was packing up on the last night of shooting is a pretty terrible way to financially doom your project. I have yet to find better rates than what Film Emporium (www.filmemporium.com) offers, personally.

> **Poor Man's Film School Sidebar:** While another week of shooting is a big deal to the broke-ass indie film production, it's pretty meaningless in the eyes of an insurer that typically deals with much longer production schedules. It likely will be of no

additional cost to have the policy cover an extra week or two beyond your anticipated wrap date – it'll be a miracle if you actually finish when you plan to – so embrace that leeway, or at least ask. Anything less than a month is probably lumped into the same premium bracket by the insurance company, but they're never going to go out of their way to let you know you could have an extra week of coverage at no cost if you don't bring it up first.

Poor Man's Film School Sidebar: If you can find a production that is finished shooting but still has an active policy that will cover your shoot dates, whether it be by word of mouth or internet-scouring that you locate it, you can try to broker a deal with the producers to allow your production to ride the coattails of their coverage. This creates additional liability for the production you're latching onto, and would absolutely be frowned upon and considered a breach of contract by the insurer, but this indie filmmaking shit isn't for the squeamish. If the producer you're negotiating with needs postproduction funds, you have some leverage in convincing them to take that risk.

:: Social Media, Marketing, Crowdfunding, Etc

Your marketing campaign does not start once the film is done. It begins the second you decide you're making the film, and you need to understand that is the current independent film marketing climate and behave accordingly if you want the film to ever find an audience. The earlier you start seeking out, wrangling that audience and, in turn, wallets receptive to monetizing this entertainment business endeavor of yours, the better. The pro forma way to go about that is establishing a social media presence and a mailing list so everyone you interact with over the course of building your production team, securing locations and casting can latch onto and keep up with the project in the fashion of their choice. If you have access to inexpensive or no-cost web design capabilities, or even better – can do it yourself on some level, securing your domain name of choice and getting a proprietary presence up on the web for your film is a crucial foundation for legitimizing the project in the eyes of all you are trying to involve at this stage (additional investors, last minute locations, crowdfunding candidates, etc.).

Some elements/functionalities of benefit in a preproduction web presence:

:: Social media links (Facebook, Twitter, YouTube) and a mailing list signup. If you have something you can give away digitally to incentivize mailing list signup, this is the platform to do it from. We offered a free mp3 track download from our soundtrack tent-pole, Des Roar, in exchange for entering your email address into a form on the website.

:: The twitter feed that will be dealing with the film should be present on the site as a short-form way of always having new content and announcements present. Ideally, you want all your facebook/twitter/blog/etc. channels to be linked together in a way that requires the minimal amount of work on your behalf when you need an update to go out on all those platforms – e.g., you can link a Twitter account directly to a specific Facebook page, and have the Twitter feed displayed on your official website, so a Twitter update is the only actual work required of you to make an announcement go out to all three. Dealing with multiple platforms for every tiny social media update gets old real fast.

> **Poor Man's Film School Sidebar:** A standalone Twitter account for the film itself is the route a lot of productions have taken in the past, and we did just that with both AGC (@agcfilm) and WWBD (@wwbd_film). In hindsight, directing all those followers to my production shingle account (@nyehentertains) would have been a much better long-term plan. In that scenario, they are then married to the creator, not just the project, who will then have access to those fans for all future projects without having to coax them over to the individual account for each new one. Individual Facebook pages are still the way to go, and each film's page can have their feeds linked directly to your production shingle Twitter account – that way all info from those Facebook sources will funnel into the one Twitter feed.

:: Contact information for whoever is handling press, investor relations and sales responsibilities for the project.

:: A preliminary press kit (The *What Would Bear Do?* press kit can be found at www.whatwouldbeardofilm.com/WWBD_Press_Kit.pdf, as an example) should be available for download.

:: A thirty second pre-pro teaser video is a great thing to have in your toolbox here as well. We shot some footage with myself and our lead actress, Jessica Kaye, for this purpose (www.youtube.com/watch?v=zMHAz8yZtco) in one afternoon at no cost, and it really helped to show the style and mood of what we were going for with the film when that question arose. As a bonus, we ended up using some of this footage in a dream sequence in the film itself, which is a lesson to always approach whatever you're doing for the project in the most professional way possible. Nothing is a throwaway in micro-budget filmmaking – you never know when an asset will be needed to help you reach your goals.

All these materials should stem from that preliminary key art design you used as your business plan cover, meaning the colors and fonts should be uniform across all materials and platforms – marketing 101 for anything you're trying to brand.

Entire books have already been written about tapping into the hot new trend of crowdfunding to finance your film, and there is a range of "crowdfunding consultants" willing to whore out their knowledge and networks to you for a price – something I believe to not be much more than a means of exploiting the pockets of overly faith-encumbered filmmakers, just as so many other entertainment side industries prey on artists. I'm of the school of thinking that a crowdfunding campaign only has reach beyond the immediate personal networks of the "owners" of a project if it has a built-in social or political agenda/movement that people can get behind and advocate. Being that I'm well-integrated into the independent filmmaking community here in New York, I'm inundated with requests for "just a few bucks" on a daily basis. If I gave to all them, I'd be back to sustaining on nothing but Lipton-brand salty rice packets like when I was in college. The campaigns I share through my social media networks and give my own money to, mostly, are the ones who are presented to me by people I have some sort of personal connection with – either they are genuine friends of mine, are artists whom I've worked with and respect, or (the selfish reason) are artists I respect and would *like* to work with. If you're going to conduct a crowdfunding campaign for a narrative project with no higher purpose than entertainment, you need to understand that you likely will only receive contributions from people who directly care about YOU – the brutal truth is very few, if any, people care about your little movie at this stage. As William Bayer put it with his trademark admirably harsh eloquence, "There's nothing so boring as an aspirant filmmaker's plight." A crowdfunding campaign is a great deal of work, and before you start off down that road you should have a realistic expectation of what it will return, and that is an expectation that should be made up solely by the immediate personal network (one degree of separation – the cousin of that girl you used to date isn't giving you any money even though you're friends on Facebook, bro) the core filmmakers have within their reach.

> **Poor Man's Film School Sidebar:** There are those who push to discount this theory by citing narrative projects that have secured relatively large sums of money without an underlying agenda beyond the simple production of the film. There are of course exceptions to every rule, but most projects fortunate

enough to achieve this without a higher cause to carry them have participants with inordinately large followings to begin with. The Brett Easton Ellis and Paul Schrader-led Kickstarter campaign for *The Canyons* was able to raise nearly $160k as merely a narrative project with no profound agenda behind it...and you probably can too if you are able to attach Ellis and Schrader to your project. If you don't have partners with 360,000+ devout twitter followers to hit up, you likely will struggle to achieve the same level of success. As a personal sidebar, I bet they would not have done nearly as well if they had informed the potential contributors they were funding a paycheck for Lindsay Lohan, who was ultimately cast as the female lead in the film.

If you're paying attention, you might have caught my use of the word "mostly" when it comes to the campaigns I take an interest in. It's more prominent in documentary projects, which by nature tend to be rooted in some real world cause or community, but when a film's subject matter encapsulates a call to action in a movement of some sort, that can lead to people's willingness to support the film as a means of supporting the higher cause. If you're putting together a documentary project about gay marriage legislation or marijuana legalization right now, you can likely tap into the existing public interest around those topics and raise money from strangers who care about those causes. Conversely, if you have a narrative project about a struggling filmmaker from the town you grew up in, fighting the odds to make it big in the movie business, you're likely going to have a rough go finding anyone other than friends and family who care enough about the project to fund it. Furthermore, that's a horrible premise for a film...but if you'd like to option the rights to it, shoot me an email.

All that realism (or potentially pessimism, according to the therapist I made up for this joke) aside, I have conducted two mildly successful IndieGogo campaigns in the past (you can pull them up at www.indiegogo.com/individuals/59612/campaigns) for small narrative projects. The *All God's Creatures* effort was for finishing funds toward the end of post, and we held a small campaign for *What Would Bear Do?* leading up to production. The latter's higher purpose was really more to "announce" the legitimacy of the project to the immediate network of those involved with the film than to raise money, which is a return from crowdfunding that is very close to, if not every bit, as much a benefit as the financial boon. A few things I learned while conducting those two campaigns:

:: It's much easier to raise money in post, when you have footage, trailers, and teasers to show from the film, than in preproduction.

:: While Kickstarter might be the more popular of the two big boys, IndieGogo is my preferred platform. The fees are lower (4% of gross funds raised vs. 5% on Kickstarter) and while the fee for it is higher (9%) you have the option of keeping the funds you raise even if the target fundraising goal is not met. The platform's interface is also more appealing to me, just from an aesthetic standpoint.

:: The "pitch video" is crucial. Its core purpose is to relay to a potential contributor why the project being funded, and ultimately produced, is important to you, but I think this sadly takes a back seat to making the video something that people want to share. This "shareability" is most easily achieved through humor, which means making the video clever in some way. With AGC, we settled on a simple direct-to-camera interview approach with the video, so we chose to play up our neediness and how little money we had spent to date on the project in hopes of achieving this. In the case of WWBD, the genre of the film being comedy made things a little easier. I had cooked up a tagline of "help us make fire, bro" for the film, so I spun that idea into basing the video around one of the characters trying, unsuccessfully, to start a fire with the old-school stick rubbing methodology. Whatever you do here, understand that a video of nothing more than you begging for money for your little movie gives someone very little incentive to share the video and ultimately reel in potential contributors from THEIR network. On the other hand, if it's something that makes people laugh, you just might attract some outside money purely because you made a stranger chuckle at their computer mid-workday.

:: Cook up a catchy tagline for the campaign, beyond what you hopefully already have for the film. That will give you some fodder to work from for the litany of social media posts and emails you will have to blast out over the course of the campaign. "help us make fire. donate." That was our tagline for the WWBD campaign, which takes little imagination to connect to the tagline for the film itself.

:: Get creative with the perks! If you pull up my two past campaigns, we offered some of the staple items (autographed scripts and DVDs, associate and executive producer credits in the film) but we peppered some things in there that were pretty fun as well, particularly with WWBD which, being a slacker buddy comedy, lent itself to oddball ideas. The two most notable items were an original set piece, an amusing mock-motivational poster that hung above the main character's couch-o-ineptitude, and a high-cost "personal appearance" perk – an offer for myself to show up and make a fire the caveman-esque, rubbing-sticks-together way, which is a play on an important plot point in the film. We did a similar "dinner cookin" offer on AGC. It seems dumb, but I have quite a few well-to-do friends who I'm confident would get a hell of a laugh out of my having to show up for either of those activities. They weren't fulfilled in either case, but if nothing else it made for something funny to read on the campaign page.

:: The ideal length for a personal funding campaign that's not pushing a social agenda of some sort, in my opinion, is thirty days. That's long enough to work your way into your immediate network's psyche, but short enough to still have the sense of urgency that a time constraint creates. Most all campaigns raise the bulk of their funds in the first and last few days of being active – extending the period in between those two likely will do very little for you.

:: Encourage sharing the campaign as much as, if not more, than you encourage people to fork over their dough. People are much more receptive to the idea of helping you share your funny video or whatever else than a direct request for cash, and are intelligent enough to ascertain your desire for fiscal contribution without you bashing them over the head with it.

:: Both Indiegogo and Kickstarter have strong analytical functionalities built into their platforms, so use them! At the very least, make sure you export those email addresses and add them to the film's mailing list.

:: Table Read

The script must be taste-tested by the actors you've cast before you get on set, and the only way to do that (other than the rehearsal you can't afford to facilitate unless your director is able to convince the actors to do it for free in a space that costs the production nothing) is at a table read. Those words will likely sound horrible as they are spoken by the end user for the first time – some of the reasons for this stem from the words being read relatively unprepared by actors sitting at a table, and others from shitty writing that has yet to be clocked and rectified. It will be the job of the writer and/or director to pick up on the particularly shitty instances and see to it they are improved upon before the start of production.

Much like the casting process, this will be an opportunity to convey the level of professionalism that the cast members are to expect in being part of your production. Organize it accordingly. Find a space that can accommodate the full cast comfortably at a large table (I've actually been to "table reads" that lacked that particular critical element) to read the script without interruption. For *All God's Creatures*, being that Matt and I were members there, we reserved a large room at the Players Club on Gramercy Park at no additional cost beyond our personal membership fees. Don't hesitate to ask around your network for access to something of similar caliber if you don't have it at your immediate disposal; the look on the faces of the cast members as they walked up the steps lined with esteemed club member's photos – actors like Tommy Lee Jones, Hal Holbrook and Kevin Spacey – was a priceless byproduct of using the venue.

Have clean, freshly printed and bound copies of the latest and greatest script waiting for them when they arrive. This can be a costly provision if you just email the job over to Kinkos and pay the standard rates, but again, poke around in your network for someone that can help out. Everyone has a friend who works a corporate office job they hate, and most people in said position are more than willing to stick it to their employer any way possible – it's the same philosophy that leads people to having massive caches of stolen office supplies they have no real need for in their home. So, be a sport and kindly allow them the opportunity to get back at their employer by way of having thirty bound copies of your baby printed and conveniently boxed for you to pick up from their office's printing division – or maybe even messengered over?

Capture video of the read, it will be useful for both script development and as bonus marketing material. Make sure there are some beverages for people to drink so anyone dying of thirst needn't interrupt the entire read to quench it. Have someone dedicated to reading the stage direction OTHER than the writer or director – they need to focus on what's working and what is not. Most of all, have fun with it. You're trying to demonstrate to these people that the time they're going to dedicate to the project, for slave labor (or less) wages, will be enjoyable and of benefit…so don't be a dick.

:: Talk to People, Ask Questions

Invariably, as you head into production, you will have unanswered questions and uncertainties that are unique to your project that no book, blog or google marathon will have a solution for. Odds are you won't be able to answer all those questions before the little red button gets pressed, but many can just by talking to people who've weathered the storm you're steering towards. If you are blessed enough to have personal connections to a filmmaker with a feature or two under their belt, or even a loose working history with one, make the effort to reach out and ask if you can buy them lunch and pick their brain a bit about the process. I worked with Ryan Gielen on a film called *The Graduates* a couple of years prior that he had done quite well with. He had since become a sort of go-to consultant in the New York independent filmmaking circuit, so I asked him if Matt and I could sit down and talk with him about some of the things he had learned while going through the process himself. We prepared a list of questions in advance to ensure we made good use of the time, and of course had many more come to mind during the meeting. Some of the topics we covered with Ryan:

> :: Ryan was particularly successful with *The Graduates* in a marketing and self-distribution capacity, so we asked a lot of questions about when and how he started those efforts.

:: Because our project was announced and listed on IMDb early in pre, and our title was *All God's Creatures*, the American Humane Association had been absolutely hounding us for weeks at this point about hiring one of their reps to oversee our shoot and ensure no animals were being mistreated – certified by the "No animals were harmed in the making of this motion picture" you often see in the end credits of a film. The only animal in our picture was a betta fish, so even if we could have afforded it we were skeptical of their thinly-veiled threats about the need for their presence. Oddly, leading up to the *What Would Bear Do?* shoot, a title every bit as insinuative of animal involvement, I didn't hear a peep out of them.

:: We were curious what his experience with distributors was on a small film with no names in it was. The answers were bleak, as they always have been and always will be.

If you don't have that luxury, use IMDb Pro to find contact info for younger filmmakers whom you admire and email them. It may be tough to get Spielberg on the horn, but you'd be surprised how receptive filmmakers are to their peers. Worst that can happen is they say no, and you need to exercise your "no receptors" anyhow, with the task of engaging distributors about a micro-budget film looming on your horizon. Feel free to email me at filmmakingthehardway@nyehentertainment.com if you think I might have the answer you need.

:: Indie Pre-Pro Legal Checklist

:: Cast contracts, with detailed nudity clauses if you're expecting that of the performer. Don't fuck it up.

:: Crew deal memos. Don't fuck it up.

:: Location agreements. Work contingency and floating additional dates into the pact whenever possible. Don't fuck it up.

:: Extra photo/voice releases. You never know when someone will end up in the shot, either by design or happenstance, and you need to have this prepared in advance and keep a slew of copies on hand at all times. You'll never get it out of them after they wander away from the set that day. Don't fuck it up.

:: Catering contract, if you are going the catering route. Don't fuck it up.

:: Production insurance policy. Don't fuck it up.

:: Shooting permits for any locations you don't have the cojones to renegade. Don't fuck it up.

:: Rental agreements for any miscellaneous rentals. Don't what? That's right – fuck it up.

:: Are You Ready?

Once all your cogs are in place, you need to call a meeting to order with your department heads – who likely are your entire departments – and go through the script page by page with them so they can air even the minutest of questions they may have. Have your assistant director run the meeting so everyone can get used to his or her management style, but of course be present and actively involved. The goal here is to eliminate, though eradicating them entirely is a lofty hope, questions popping up during production that you don't have answers to. You'll have no time to concoct clever and cost-effective solutions once production starts, so do everything in your power to minimize the wizardry required of you.

Do you know where your power sources, holding and bathroom facilities will be for each location, and do you have both a primary and backup food option for each one of them? Call the contact person associated with each and verbally confirm the dates, times and locations they will be needed. Do the same with your actors. Do the same with your crew members. Have you worked every kink out of the script? Have you shot-listed and/or storyboarded your days sufficiently? Have you thought of every single possible scenario and two contingency plans for each, should they go awry?

Ok, good. Now go back and do all that checking again, and then let's make a goddamn movie. Don't fuck it up.

CUT TO:

Production

The following is a day-to-day recount of the *All God's Creatures* sixteen-day shooting schedule that took place from March 1st, 2010 through March 20th, 2010.

:: Day 0

In true pompous indie filmmaker fashion, we originally scheduled the start of the shoot for February 14th – Valentine's Day. We were, after all, shooting a movie about a love story, and that symbolism "spoke to us as artists." Two weeks prior to that, around the first of February, Ryan and Frank asked for a meeting where they requested that Matt and I push the start date back to March 1st. They cited a number of reasons, most of them dealing with simple creative preparation needs. We were resistant to the delay, holding our death grip on the "let's just fucking do this" mentality that we felt had gotten us to the doorstep of production in the first place, but we eventually relented and accommodated their request. Whether it was of creative benefit to the film is open to debate, but it did turn out to be a wise decision from a physical production standpoint – the 11th and 12th of the month brought about the biggest snow storm in NYC history, with snowfall accumulation reports in the ballpark of 26 inches. Transportation and parking were a nightmare, businesses we would have depended on were closed, and many cast and crew were probably still tunneling out of their apartments. Because we listened, the film gods were seemingly in our corner.

Other than the aforementioned loss of the coffee shop location, and the scrambling required to replace that loss, the days leading up to the actual start date of the shoot were relatively uneventful. I'd like to attribute that to our meticulous planning and attention to detail, but it probably was just another instance of those film gods smiling down on us. Your mindset for the final approach to the start of production should be the following: no matter how much planning and preparation you put in, shit will go wrong. Be ready to fix it.

:: Day 1 :: March 1st, 2010 :: 5.125 Pages

When scheduling a film shoot, a seasoned line producer will usually speak with the director about potential scene options in an effort to keep the subject matter light on the first day of shooting. Because you are bringing a large group of people together for the first time in what will inevitably be a tenuous work environment, it's a wise choice to arrange your schedule in a way that allows for you to ease into the flow of working together with something simple. We did not know or think of that, and instead scheduled a crucial first date scene with the two lead characters – in other words, subject matter that is <u>entirely</u> predicated on chemistry between those two characters. We did this because it was a bar location we had total control over, and we felt that was reason enough to start there without even considering the implications on the quality of the footage we would get. It was also the location for a scene (ultimately a scene we cut) between me and a character we cast with my co-producer Matt – another example of self-serving filmmaker symbolism. The day fortunately worked out overall, due in large part to the talent and professionalism of our lead actress

(Jessica Kaye), but had we known then what we know now we would never have scheduled those scenes for day one.

The way we were able to secure the location, as previously mentioned, was because I worked in the bar. Being that there was no way we could afford to shut the bar down during business hours, we were looking at an overnight shoot that started when the bar closed at 4 AM after a predictably slow Sunday night – that I bartended the ten hours of prior to the start of that shooting. Not exactly the ideal preparation for your lead actor's first day of work, but if you're a main cog in a low-budget filmmaking machine, that's the kind of sacrifice necessary to keep the wheels greased. After having logged many a Sunday night behind an empty bar from three to four AM, we knew we could set the crew call at three and loaded in for that last hour of business.

A bar location of course needed some extras, which we couldn't afford to pay – and money is one of the few reasons anyone is interested in sitting around for hours as an extra. This is where you start calling in favors from friends. Matt called some actor friends he knew, I called some non-actor friends I know, and we used a few of the crew members – unrecognizably positioned because you'll need to use them a number of times on the fly during the shoot. Even with all that legwork, and shot with tight framing to minimize the reveal of the empty space around the characters, the location still looked sparsely populated.

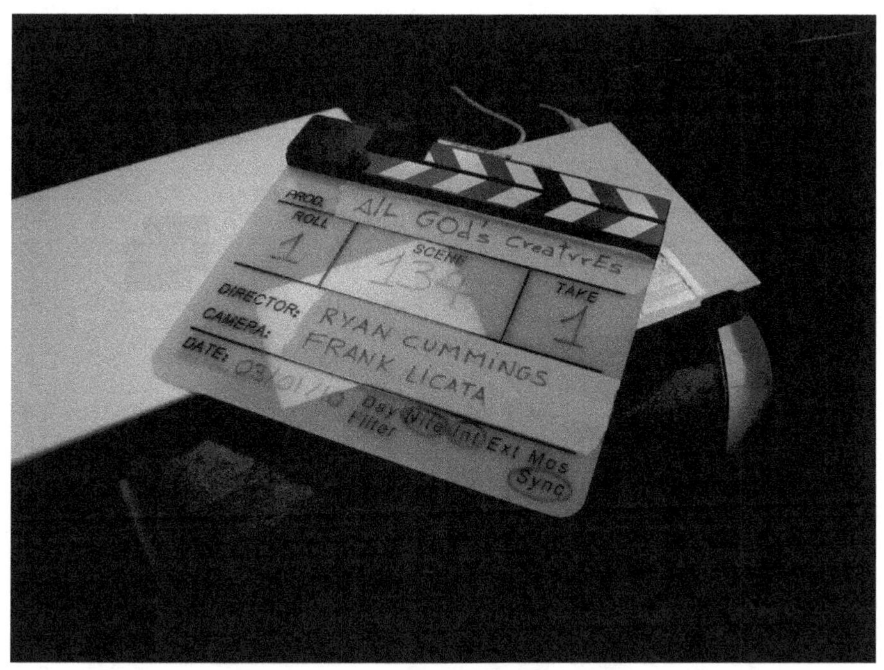

The Slate, Day 1

The bar would reopen again at ten AM, which gave us six hours to knock out two pretty substantial scenes. We pulled it off, sent everyone home except me, Ryan, Frank and Matt (which allowed us to skip buying lunch) and then wrapped up the day with some MOS daytime exteriors of me walking around NYC streets. All in all, it could have been a shit-ton worse.

:: Day 2 :: March 2nd, 2010 :: 4.375 Pages

The subway scene called for another overnight shoot, which jived with our previous day running the same late-night hours. If you're going to shoot on a train line, particularly a very busy train line, it need be done during the lowest-traffic period for that train line. The low volume stint we chose for our train line was 3 AM on a Tuesday morning. We pared our crew down to just the co-directors/cinematographer, piled the unused actors and crew onto one end of the empty car and shot the direction opposite them. The only sound we were able to capture was camera sound, rationalized by the plan to lay voiceover in its place. Needing a second kind of train setting for two later occurrences of train travel in the script, we had to move our skeleton operation to another type of train and do it all over again later in the morning. Less than six hours of shooting, so no lunch. Short day of renegade film production, no major hiccups.

We were so pleased with how the first couple of days had went, we decided to give all crew members not being paid a day rate a quarter point of the net on the film as a token of our appreciation for their hard work. If your crew is busting their ass for you, find a way to show them you see and appreciate it.

:: Day 3 :: March 3rd, 2010 :: 9.625 Pages

The first day of four consecutive we would be spending shooting in my apartment at the time - pretty much the most excruciating experience of my anal-retentive, type-A existence. If you value the space you live in, avoid bringing a production in to shoot there at all costs. It was good to get that off my chest, thanks for listening.

We had a bit of a scheduling conundrum when it came to the serial killer's bedroom. The first half of the story required it to have a disturbing, distressed look to it (body parts saved in jars of formaldehyde, girl's pictures and locks of severed hair tacked up all over the place, a crazy paint job on the walls) that called for quite a bit of work by our art department, and then around the story's midpoint the room is cleaned up and restored to relative normalcy. That meant we'd have to either distress the room to start and make sure it was cleaned and repainted in time to shoot the post-cleaning scenes, or shoot the clean scenes first and do the distressing before shooting the earlier scenes. Further complicating the situation was my need to physically live in this apartment while all this was going on. We decided the latter situation was best, which meant we'd shoot out the clean bedroom scenes on the first day at the location and move out to the living room while Jennifer and Victor worked to demonize the bedroom.

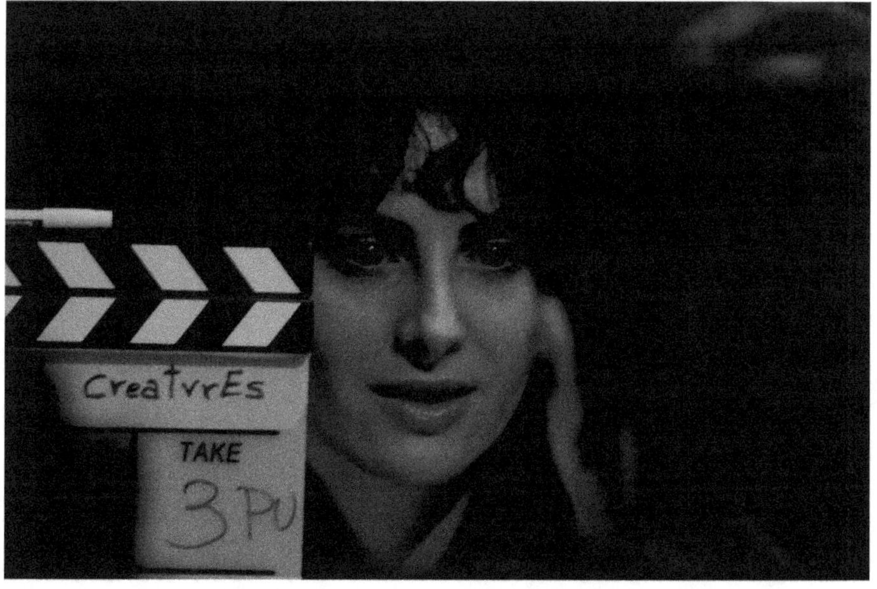

Delia [Jessica Kaye]

We started with a number of relatively simple solo interiors with me for the first half of the day, and then tackled a big fight scene and the lone sex scene in the film after our lead actress came in around the meal break – the first of many Subway sandwich lunches we would have. In any production setting requiring nudity of the actors, extra steps need be taken to convey management's effort to ensure a safe and private environment. A micro-budget production should go above and beyond those expectations, as even the most inexperienced actor is going to have apprehensions about putting themselves in such a vulnerable position for a project lacking professional-level amenities and provisions, as any production in this budget tier will. If you want believable intimacy to come out of this type of material, you'll need to quell every possible concern your talent might have leading up to it. As mentioned in the casting notes on this topic, we made sure to schedule some dedicated rehearsal time where we could go over, shot to shot, what would be covered while shooting these scenes in a fully-clothed and comfortable setting. We closed the set down and made sure the crew was as minimalistic as possible, scheduled more time for these scenes than the page count would normally warrant, and made sure to provide robes between takes. It made for a late night, but we did it right and it went smoothly.

:: Day 4 :: March 4th, 2010 :: 3.75 Pages

With the previous day going long, a difficult day five on the schedule after this, and the bedroom distressing job needing to be finished, we planned for this to be a short day. Some easy solo stuff with my character, a post-dinner scene with Jessica and I that was the lead-in for what we shot the day before, had a Subway lunch break, then we packed up and headed down to the deli on the corner to shoot the claw machine scene.

Seeing as we were offering nothing to the location (other than making some coffee and small crafty purchases) in exchange for the opportunity to shoot there, we had no grounds to ask them to disrupt their business to accommodate our needs. That meant the Spanish Harlem locals that were meandering in and around the store became our extras for the evening whether we liked it or not. Luckily, they were cool about doing as we asked, which included signing off on photo releases (which you should always have plenty of on-hand in your production bible). One of them, in what is likely the most awkward and out-of-place background appearances in film history, can be spotted sitting in an old office chair that was on the corner amongst some discarded furniture while clearly focusing his attention on watching us film the scene. Other than that, and the good natured but not-so-useful ideas that our impromptu extras kept offering up between takes, it was a well-executed day of shooting.

:: Day 5 :: March 5th, 2010 :: 7.25 Pages

Back into my apartment for a bunch of solo stuff with my character and some heavier material involving the last of Jon's murders in the script. We had to shuffle the plan for the day a little bit to accommodate the art team finishing up the bedroom a little later than the ridiculous timeline we tried imposing on them, but it worked out.

We had another instance calling for a closed set - a topless scene we were asking of Molly Fahey, which we were sure to approach with the same level of accommodation we had with Jessica's two nights prior. Despite that and the day running about twelve hours, another

Subway lunch that led to the first noticeable grumbles about the emerging pattern was probably the most arduous part of the day.

:: Day 6 :: March 6th, 2010 :: 8 Pages

In what I thought would be the last day of angst-filled occupancy of my apartment by the production, we had a 17-hour day in front of us with two effects-filled, bloody kills on the schedule. The first was a screwdriver stabbing of the character played by Ginger Kroll that was the crucial, tone-setting opener for the film, the second a meat tenderizer bludgeoning of a prostitute played by Christy Prais. From the outset, we intended to keep the gore aspects of the serial killer's practices to a minimum. Two reasons for this; one, while the film happened to center around a killer and a prostitute, it was important to us that the audience be focused on the love story developing between them, and not the sex and murder. Two, we didn't have the money to facilitate elaborate effects. Keep it simple, keep it simple.

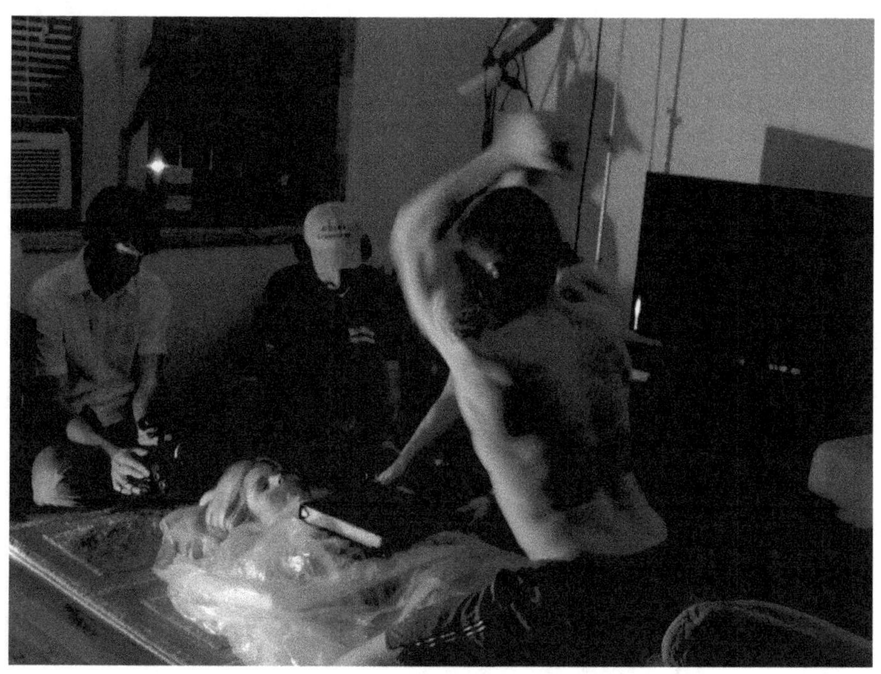

Safely executing a stabbing with actress Ginger Kroll

For the screwdriver stabbing, we had a mannequin torso that was precut with a small hole in the sternum area and had our makeup artist load it with a stage blood packet. The killer, being meticulously clean, would wrap his victims in clear plastic painting drop cloths as a means of minimizing the mess, so we wrapped the mannequin in one of those and shot ECU's of the head of the screwdriver piercing the plastic and being pulled out covered in blood. That, cut together with CU's of the actress' face having blood flicked on it, as well as a reverse of my face having the same done to it while I plunged the screwdriver down out of frame towards the "body," is how we sold the stabbing in the edit.

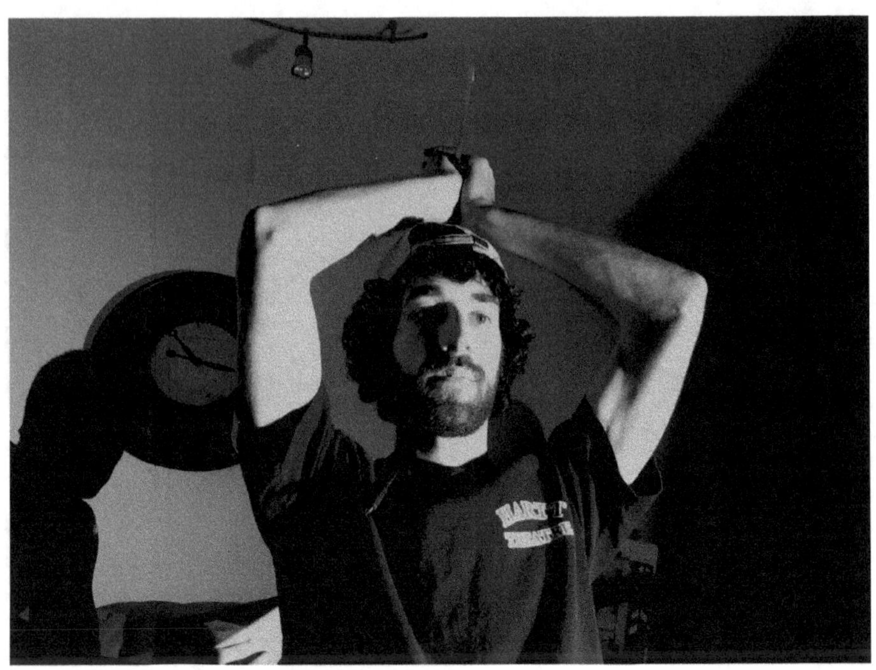

Co-director Ryan Charles showing me how it's done

The second murder was written to be a lot more gruesome than we decided we were fiscally capable of, originally being the aforementioned meat tenderizer assault, followed by the ripping of the victim's eye from its socket. The eye effect proved to be too much for both of our gore-oriented philosophies for the film, so we cut it. We sold the initial strike with the meat tenderizer in an over-the-shoulder shot on Christy, me approaching her from behind and swinging the tenderizer towards her as she turned into it – plenty of physical space between the two of us to safely do so. That angle took us to the instant the tenderizer "made contact," with accompanying cringe-worthy sound effect, after which we cut to a soft-focus pan from behind of me, hunched over Christy, manically beating her with the tenderizer.

We also had the first of many direct-to-camera interview scenes that both lead characters had in the script I wrote on the schedule. They were written as black and white, surrealistic moments that followed particularly tenuous moments in the script – murders with Jon, instances of prostitution with Delia. A lot of the dialogue incorporated quotes from actual serial killers and prostitutes I was able to mine from a number of internet-based sources during the writing process. My co-producer Matt and I felt that these were integral factors in getting the audience inside the minds of the lead characters, as well as helped to achieve the overall dark feel we thought the film should have. The directors, on the other hand, felt they slowed the narrative and didn't care for them. As a result, they put minimal planning, and probably even less effort, into shooting them. Who was right or wrong is moot at this point, but it no doubt would be a much darker film with those included. What is also certain is that without the proper attention and effort paid to shooting them, we did not have solid enough footage on the material to have the option of seeing how they would work in the editing room – something I regret.

Poor Man's Film School Sidebar: With all the work required to get into production, you are doing yourself a major disservice if you leave anything on the table while you're there. If you want something, you have to fight for it – or spend post-production and beyond wondering what could have been. Reshoots are hard to come by even in adequately-funded production settings, your chances of making them happen in micro-budget filmmaking is sparse at best...so get what you want the first time around.

Two Subway meals, crew very unhappy with it.

:: Day 7 :: March 8th, 2010 :: 6.375 Pages

Hotel Caribe on 145th Street in Harlem was the setting for the seedy motel Delia would service her clients (played by Tym Moss & Daniel Angus Cox) in, which we commandeered overnight for the cost of one room rental – about $90 for the night. They even allowed us to store equipment and shoot in the lobby (including the bullet-proof glass-protected attendant booth, which they let us flick lit cigarettes at) and hallways.

We finished there in five hours or so and moved over to a short comedic relief scene hysterically carried by Richard Jordan at a small Mexican/Pizza (interesting hybrid, no?) takeout joint a few blocks away on Broadway. The crew was ecstatic with our payment arrangement for the location, which was buying dinner there the night of – which meant no Subway. Rejoice. Tough to say whether it was just the change of pace or actually a case of tasty cuisine, but it went over quite well and we ordered there a few times more over the course of shoot. I believe it was even cheaper than Subway, so no complaints from the accounting department.

:: Day 8 :: March 9th, 2010 :: 3.875 Pages

Out to Staten Island, where we would be invading Frank & Ryan's Aunt's house to convert it into the Maitlin household for two days. The 1st half of the day would be a slew of solo phone call scenes with Tiffany Lee, who played the younger sister of Kaye's character, the second half a highly sensitive rape scene that required even more care than the sex scenes we shot back at my apartment. The crew was scaled back to its minimum again, again we set aside considerably more time than the page count would normally require, and even we the producers cleared out to allow for the privacy necessary to handle this subject matter. I think it turned out to be one of the more powerful moments in the film, as well as one of the closest adherences to what I wrote long before we ever got together to make this movie. I found it interesting how many times that was not the case, simply because the words were being filtered through other minds (the co-directors) and financial constraints (our limited budget) as they were carried out. This was not necessarily a bad thing, as there were a lot of fresh ideas that ended up in the film that were not in the script as a result, it was an interesting and growing experience going through the process as a screenwriter for the first time nonetheless.

Had a hard time finding a Subway near the neighborhood we were shooting in, so it was pizza for dinner. Again, the crew was stoked.

:: Day 9 :: March 10th, 2010 :: 3.5 Pages

Second day at the house on Staten Island, shooting all of the Delia scenes. We were fortunate enough to have a friend who had his own HVX camera and agreed to come out and be a second camera operator for a few days of our shoot, which allowed for us to blow through our coverage by shooting both angles/actors at the same time.

With that luxury, we were able make our day in relatively short time despite some heavy subject matter. We were also able to eventually find a Subway for sandwiches, so as not to spoil our five dollar footlong-beleaguered crew.

:: Day 10 :: March 11th, 2010 :: 6 Pages

Back into Manhattan, up to the "production office" that also was the setting for Delia's studio apartment – Matt's living room – to shoot a number of solo scenes with Jessica. We also used his bathroom to shoot all the Maitlin household bathroom scenes, which was much more suitable for our camera angle needs than the house on Staten Island.

> **Poor Man's Film School Sidebar:** For some bizarre reason I am often inclined to keep filming locations matched with their real world surroundings, and it's a completely pointless tendency. The audience will never, ever be able to deduce that one bathroom isn't the bathroom that is actually in the house it's portrayed as being set in, as long as you shoot smart.

Things were looking good, budget-wise, so we splurged on some Chinese food for dinner.

:: Day 11 :: March 12th, 2010 :: 1.625 Pages

We were originally scheduled to shoot a few exteriors down in Riverbank Park around 148th Street, but rainy weather forced us to push that to another day and swap in some leftover interiors in Delia's apartment that we had scheduled on the 18th. We also had a short and simple restaurant interior that was nearby Matt's apartment, so we were able to keep that. The change created a very hectic day of shooting for us the following Thursday, but that was a corner we backed ourselves into by not having those exteriors scheduled early enough to have ample interior rescheduling options left on the slate. It did however make for a short day here, and no one on the cast and crew ever complains about that no matter how detrimental it may be in the long run.

:: Day 12 :: March 13th, 2010 :: 7.5 Pages

The first of our coffee shop days. The shop would close at 9 PM and reopen at 6 AM, so our window of opportunity on any one day was limited to that stretch. We had issues with noise from a number of the coolers and other pieces of equipment in the location which, even after we did what we could to quiet them, would leave us with subpar sound to work with in post.

> **Poor Man's Film School Sidebar:** When you unplug or turn a piece of equipment off that puts perishable foodstuffs or something like that at risk, such as a refrigerator, a great way to remember to plug it back in before you leave is to stash your car keys (or something else you can't leave the location without) inside it. If you are able to get a business owner to do you a solid, letting you shoot there, and you burn hundreds of dollars of his inventory because it spoils in an unplugged cooler you forgot to plug back in, you're going to have a pissed off owner on your hands. It's very important that you never burn your

bridges when there's no money to construct new ones. If being a decent human being in general isn't inclination enough, you may need to come back and reshoot something at some point – and that will not be going down if trash their place the first time you're there. Also, you never want to create any unnecessary bad mojo on an indie film project.

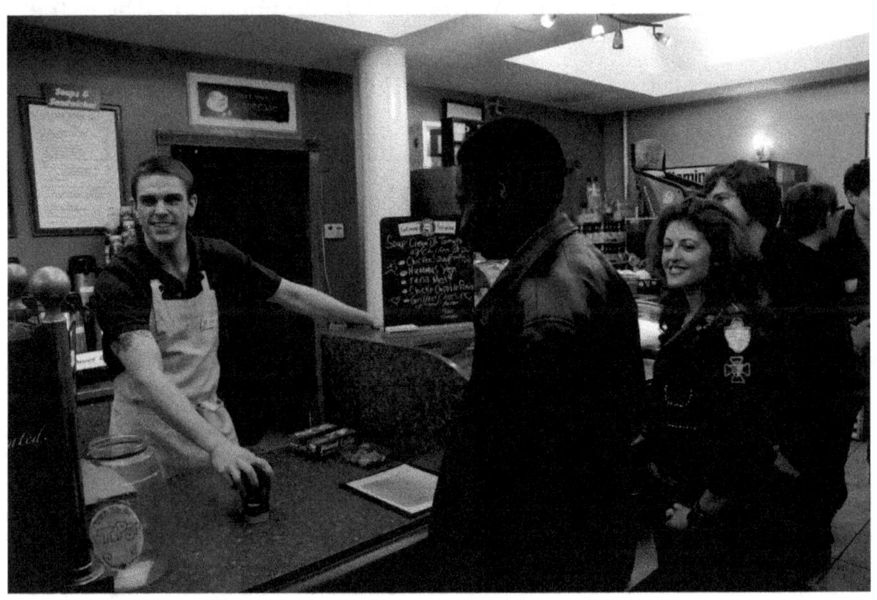

Jon at the coffee shop with our extras

For both of these coffee shop days we had needs for extras that required hours beyond what you could ask a friend to put in for you for free, so even with Matt's extensive actor database fully tapped we had to turn to a Craigslist ad to get some people there. One, Travis Del Valle, was even awarded the opportunity for a line of dialogue – the holy grail of an actor doing extra work. We also awarded on-screen credit to the other extras willing to pull the overnighter for us, given the absence of pay, which is something not normally allotted to a background player.

Poor Man's Film School Sidebar: One of our scenes with Delia here called for her to be perusing Craigslist ads for jobs, which is where she stumbles onto the idea of prostitution. We wanted to make our own ad, which I did by modifying the HTML (an easy task if you have any HTML experience whatsoever, given Craigslist's simplicity) on an actual personals listing of theirs.

The owner of the shop was seemingly pretty excited about a film being shot in his store, one of the main reasons he allowed us to shoot there at all, and likely wanted to make sure we weren't tearing the place up, so he stuck around the entire time we were shooting there. They had a nice food menu, so for our meal break we gave the crew a choice between ordering from there (which the owner offered to prepare) and ordering from a Chinese takeout joint across the street. Because Jessica Kaye and I both had worked on the New York-based soap operas (*One Life to Live* and *All My Children*) I was able to convince a friend of mine who was an editor at Soap Digest to come check out the shoot, and we conducted an interview with him during the break as well.

Poor Man's Film School Sidebar: Press is VERY hard to come by for small productions with no name recognition, so make sure to tap as many personal connections as you can to drive interest to the production – an offer that is most attractive to journalists during the excitement of the shoot. Strike while the iron is hot, as they say. And stuff.

Because our time allotment at the café was so short, we also scheduled an hour to get the quick MOS movie theater scene we had at the Abingdon Theatre in midtown.

:: Day 13 :: March 14th, 2010 :: 7.75 Pages

The second day of coffee shop shooting was set to start with a different location also – an employment agency Delia visits in her NYC job search. Being that we were in the midst of an eye-of-the-hurricane-esque multi-day run without any major hiccups, we were due for some catastrophe. It played out as follows:

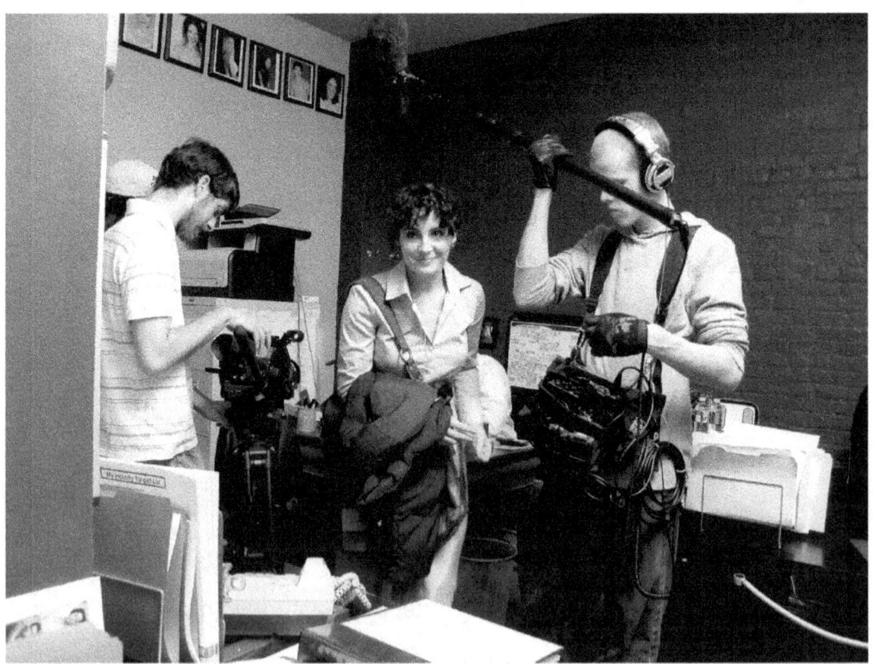

Delia pursues employment

I woke up that day – basically amounting to later in the night of the day prior because we had been shooting till 5 AM – to a voicemail from our contact for that evening's office location informing me that we were no longer going to be able to shoot there for some (blasphemous for me at the time, but probably quite founded) reason. Good morning to you, producer. No worries though, we had a backup location – the office of Matt's day job at the time. One phone call to him, this crisis will be averted. I make the call, straight to voicemail. Again, same thing. Again. Again. Again. Voicemail. I would later find out he had turned his phone off after making sure all of the next day's ducks were in a row while he got some much needed shut-eye. I've met his boss a few times, so I try giving the office a call. The man of the hour isn't in, the receptionist is unsure of how to handle the situation and is clueless as to when he'll be back, so I leave a message. I don't have his cell. Or do I? I think I may have gotten his business card at some point...maybe. It is definitely not in my contacts on my phone. A mad dash home from the gym, followed by a desperate rifling through my box-o-cocktail-party-fodder, turns up what in my eyes was the most valuable piece of Vistaprint-watermarked pseudo cardstock on the planet that afternoon. I get him on the horn, hammer out the particulars, and my producing partner wakes up to a lineage of voicemails that likely took him through an entire emotional spectrum over the course of a few minutes but ended in good news: we are on schedule and under budget.

Poor Man's Film School Sidebar: ALWAYS have one contingency plan, strive for having two. ALWAYS have detailed documentation of every minute detail pertaining to them, and ALWAYS make sure every decision maker on the production has all of this information on-hand at all times.

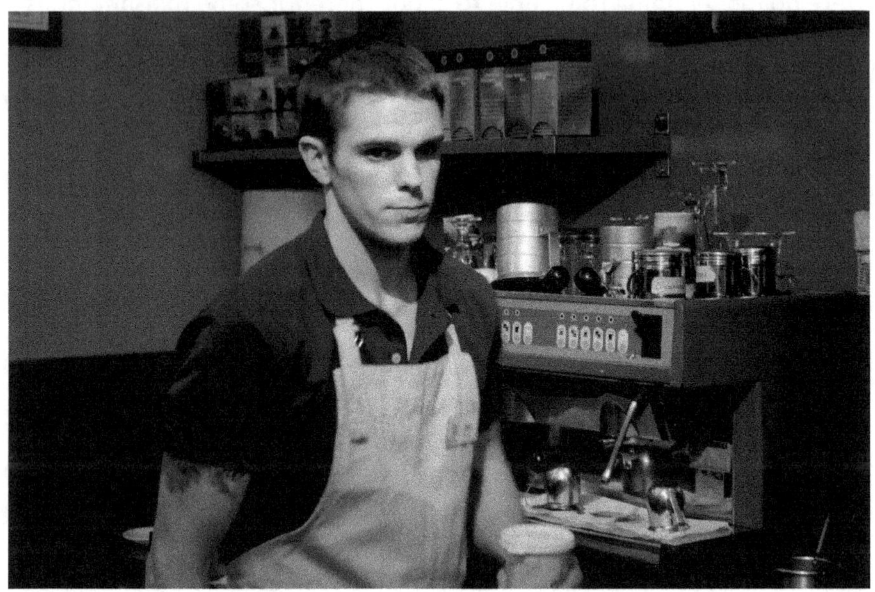

The barista

So we got that office stuff and headed up to the coffee shop. While we were able to get "through" all the scenes on the schedule, we did not have the time to properly cover them and would inevitably be back over the summer for a night of reshooting.

:: Day 14 :: March 18th, 2010 :: 11.875 Pages

A nightmare schedule. We started at nightfall with some alleyway exteriors behind Matt's apartment, then moved out front of the building for two contrasting, dialogue-heavy scenes with Ginger Kroll and Jessica Kaye both interacting with my character at the end of dates. As previously stated, Matt's building was on W. 145th Street in

Harlem, which isn't as busy on a Thursday night as a midtown street perhaps is, but it was by no means quiet – nowhere in Manhattan is. Matt, having lived there for a couple of years at this point, had developed a rapport with some Crips (the gang that for all intents and purposes oversaw the block) that lived in his building. They were quite interested in the shoot taking place on their block and, despite some mild concern amongst a few of the more tightly-wound cast and crew, ended up being a great ally for the evening – even shutting down traffic on the street during takes.

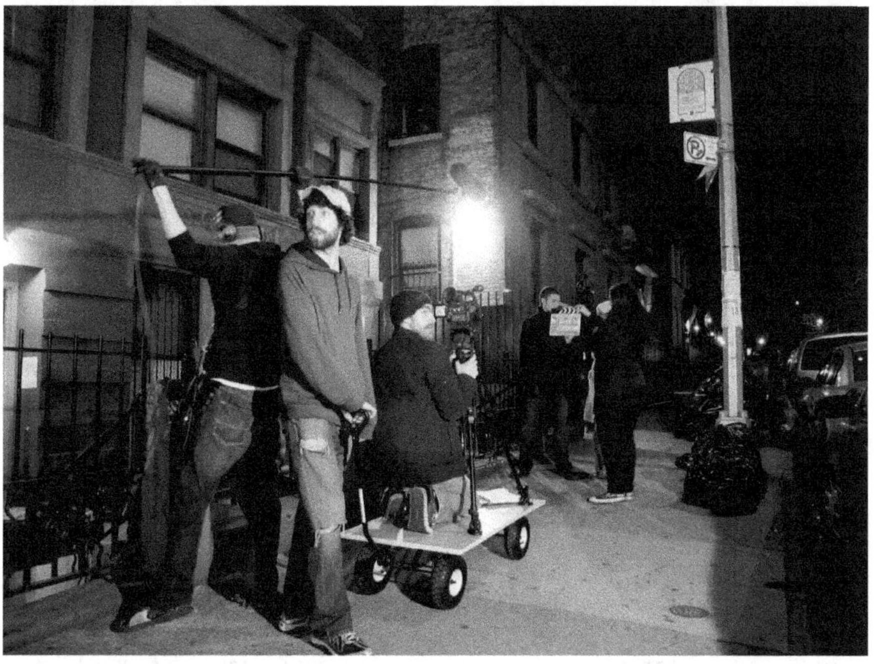

Indie filmmaking at its finest

From there it was down to Riverside Park to make up for the rain day we had experienced the week prior. This required lugging a massive Home Depot generator from the street, down the network of steps and overpasses required to reach the riverbank the shooting locations were on, and an even more painstaking experience lugging it back up later once we were done. We started with a strangulation scene on a park bench with actress Cat Johnson, beautifully set in front of the George Washington Bridge, and then moved on to a body disposal scene at the river itself.

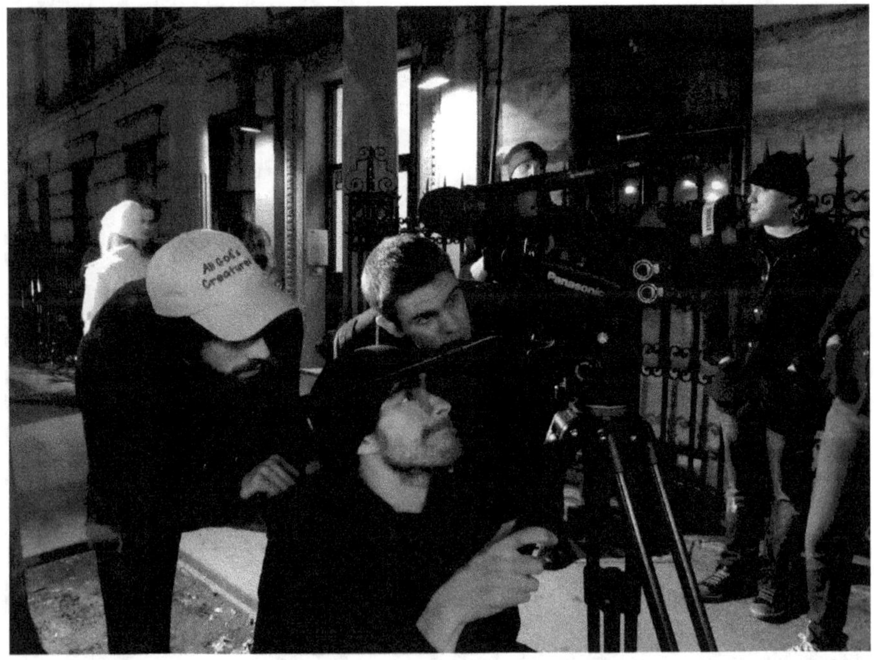

Lining up the shot

Because run-of-the-mill Home Depot generators (as opposed to those intended for production, which operate with far less racket) are inherently loud, we were forced to set it far off in the distance from where we were shooting and run extension cable to the lighting. A little short on available hands, director Ryan Charles was at one point off by the generator holding a sound blanket in front of it so we could get clean (or at least semi-clean) sound capture – a prime example of the "everyone does everything" mentality required of all participants on a micro-budget film crew.

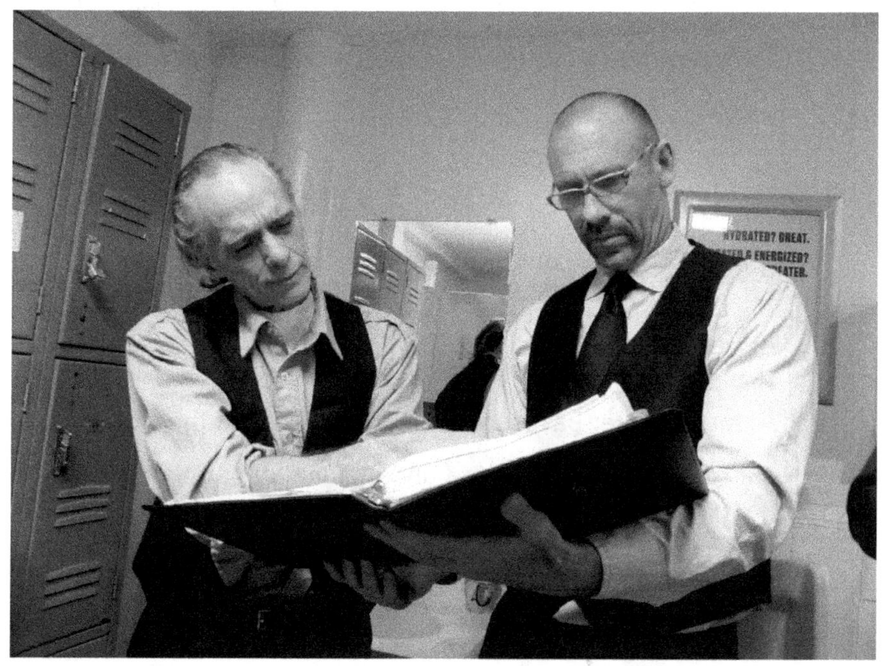

Don [Carson Grant] and Sean [Adam Barnett] study their lines

From there it was back up to the production office area, where we had arranged to enter a 24-hour gym on Broadway at around 3 AM – their slowest time period – to shoot the "Amtrak employee break room" scene between Adam Barnett and Carson Grant in their locker room. We would come to realize the next afternoon the P2 card (the HVX camera storage media) that the last of Carson's coverage was shot on was corrupt – a terrifying realization when you can't afford to go back to a location. In yet another of the film gods' kind moments, it turned out that Carson had nailed it on the second take of his coverage – the last scene filmed before switching over to the corrupt storage media. He even ad-libbed a line at the end of the scene that encapsulated the entire film – "And in between all the shit, Sean, every once and a while there's a good moment. You'll find yours." Calling that brilliant acting work doesn't even begin to broach how we feel about that clutch performance.

:: Day 15 :: March 19th, 2010 :: 3.5 Pages

Though the page count was low, at least relative to some of what we had been up against over the course of the shoot, the film's climax in the rail yard was all action and called for a hell of a night. We were shooting in Oyster Bay – about an hour outside of the city on Long Island – our most daunting logistical undertaking of the shoot by far. We had to round everyone up and head out in time to stop at their town hall of sorts to obtain our $500 shooting permit by 5 PM when it closed, get settled at the Railroad Museum (www.obrm.org) to do an interview with the local newspaper (www.oysterbayguardian.com), and map out our shot list in the yard before the sun went down.

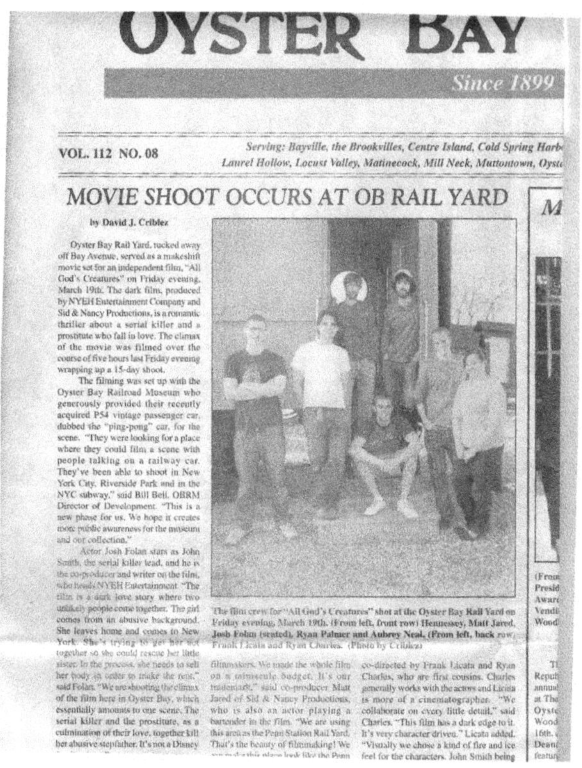

OYSTER BAY

Since 1899

VOL. 112 NO. 08

Serving: Bayville, the Brookvilles, Centre Island, Cold Spring Harb
Laurel Hollow, Locust Valley, Matinecock, Mill Neck, Muttontown, Oyst

MOVIE SHOOT OCCURS AT OB RAIL YARD

by David J. Criblez

Oyster Bay Rail Yard, tucked away off Bay Avenue, served as a makeshift movie set for an independent film, "All God's Creatures" on Friday evening, March 19th. The dark film, produced by NYEH Entertainment Company and Sid & Nancy Productions, is a romantic thriller about a serial killer and a prostitute who fall in love. The climax of the movie was filmed over the course of five hours last Friday evening wrapping up a 15-day shoot.

The filming was set up with the Oyster Bay Railroad Museum who generously provided their recently acquired P54 vintage passenger car, dubbed the "ping-pong" car, for the scene. "They were looking for a place where they could film a scene with people talking on a railway car. They've been able to shoot in New York City, Riverside Park and in the NYC subway," said Bill Bell, OBRM Director of Development. "This is a new phase for us. We hope it creates more public awareness for the museum and our collection."

Actor Josh Folan stars as John Smith, the serial killer lead, and he is the co-producer and writer on the film, who heads NYEH Entertainment. "The film is a dark love story where two unlikely people come together. The girl comes from an abusive background. She leaves home and comes to New York. She's trying to get her act together so she could rescue her little sister. In the process, she needs to sell her body in order to make the rent," said Folan. "We are shooting the climax of the film here in Oyster Bay, which essentially amounts to one scene. The serial killer and the prostitute, as a culmination of their love, together kill her abusive stepfather. It's not a Disney

The film crew for "All God's Creatures" shot at the Oyster Bay Rail Yard on Friday evening, March 19th. (From left, front row) Hennessey, Matt Jared, Josh Folan (seated), Ryan Palmer and Aubrey Neal. (From left, back row) Frank Licata and Ryan Charles. (Photo by Criblez)

filmmakers. We made the whole film on a minuscule budget. It's our trademark," said co-producer Matt Jared of Sid & Nancy Productions, who is also an actor playing a bartender in the film. "We are using this area as the Penn Station Rail Yard. That's the beauty of filmmaking! We

co-directed by Frank Licata and Ryan Charles, who are first cousins. Charles generally works with the actors and Licata is more of a cinematographer. "We collaborate on every little detail," said Charles. "This film has a dark edge to it. It's very character driven," Licata added. "Visually we chose a kind of fire and ice feel for the characters. John Smith being

Oyster Bay Guardian article

Poor Man's Film School Sidebar: Small towns are usually pretty easy to excite over the invasion of a film production, regardless of how small the scope of that production may be, which means convincing the local press outlets to do a piece on your film shouldn't be all that difficult. Never pass up press of any kind, so pick up the phone and get the editor on the phone. As close-knit as small towns can be, you never know what kind of production benefits the local press staff may be able to line up.

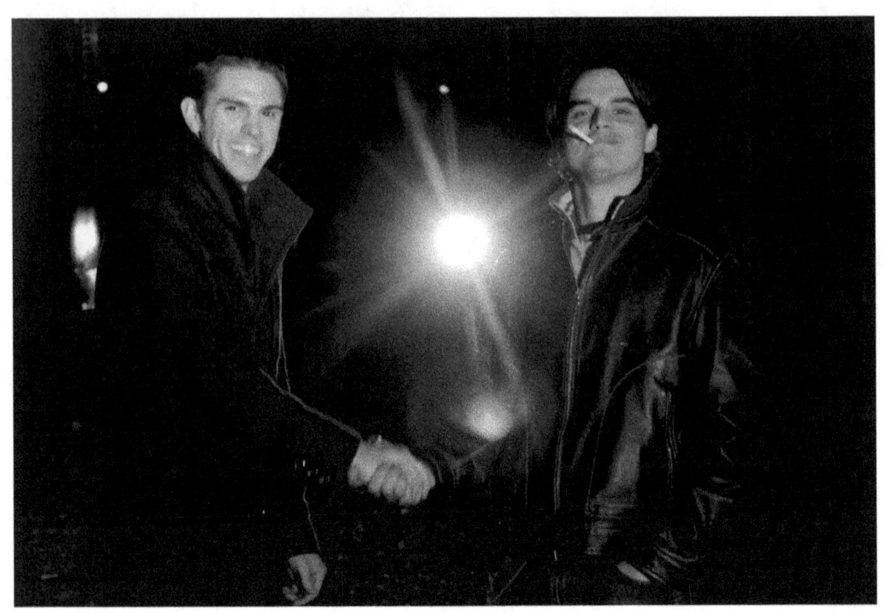

Victorious producers

Other than it being quite cold, there weren't many setbacks. The biggest drag on our schedule was an issue one of our actors had with smoking cigarettes – he didn't express any issue with doing so in advance, which we were certain to responsibly clear with him before the start of the shoot, but after doing a few takes of a scene with him trying to produce as much smoke as possible for the camera's benefit, he became ill. It took about 45 minutes for him to get himself back together. Whenever he and I speak, even years after the fact now, cigarette jokes are exchanged without fail.

We did avoid some financial complication at the start of the day. In our negotiations with the museum's lawyer, it was agreed we would give them a $1000 check as a deposit for the location (in addition to our insurance, which of course had a deductible) in case our presence resulted in any damages. It would be returned within two weeks after the shoot date as long as everything was in order after our departure. A more than reasonable request, but it turned out to be one we really couldn't afford. Whether conscious or not (though I suspect it was, out of kindness – the shaving consultant chuckle influence, perhaps?), the museum curator, Bill Bell, never requested the deposit check. This would turn out be a great thing, as once all the debit card transactions had balanced out after the hysteria of our last few days, there would not have been sufficient funds in our operating account to cover it. Film gods.

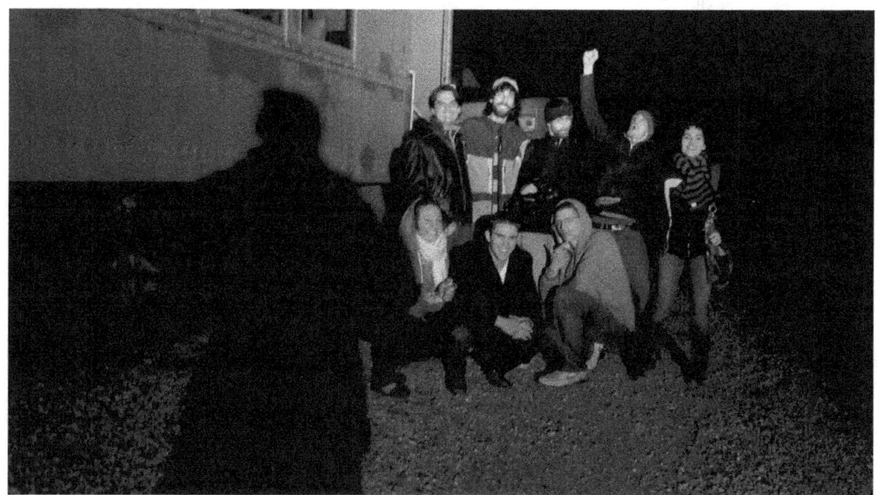

It's a wrap!

Before we left, we were sure to take our wrap photo – don't forget this little gem. Finishing your first feature with mere tuppence for a budget is a moment you'll want to hang on your penthouse office wall somewhere down the line.

:: Day 16 :: March 20th, 2010 :: 4.375 Pages

We had a few leftover shots that didn't fit into anywhere in particular on the schedule, as well as some leftover stuff we didn't get to satisfactorily at my apartment in the four days we were there, so we decided to tack on an extra day to grab all that. We took our time with it, so it developed into a fairly full day of shooting.

One thing we didn't properly plan out was the winding down of the production – equipment and vehicle return, art department fallout, etc. At the end of the full day of shooting, which we didn't really plan for it to be at the outset, the production van needed to go back to CC Rental downtown. Matt had been out running errands for the production most of the day, I had been on set working. It didn't occur to us until afterwards that one of us would have to drop people and equipment off and return the van. The decision making process to decide who's rightful responsibility this was became a daddy-hit-mommy-at-the-dinner-table-like argument in front of the entire crew as they silently loaded out the equipment; Doors slamming, hysterical things being said, the whole scope. Looking back, it was a hilarious punctuation mark on the shoot that didn't amount to anything more than blowing off the steam built up over the course of the last three weeks, but it wouldn't have happened if we had properly delineated the wrap-up responsibilities in advance.

:: Indie Production Legal Checklist

:: The goal of a well thought out pre-pro period is to line up all the dominoes well enough that you needn't deal with this tedious shit once they start falling, but you'll inevitably have a couple that don't. A little producer trick you can do to make sure you don't forget to knock those stubborn ones down at the appropriate time is to take a look at the shooting scene breakdown each morning, which should have all production elements (actors, extras, props, locations) going on camera that day listed. Go through them one by one and physically cross each off after you've double checked having all the appropriate paperwork in place for it.

:: Decompression Limbo

Despite the urge you'll have to start sifting through your footage and assembling the film, take a week or two off before doing so. You deserve it, and you'll be in a better mindset for the post-production gauntlet after that clearing of the mechanism.

CUT TO:

Post-Production

Post Checklist

:: Rough Picture Assembly

:: Re-Shoots

:: Picture Lock

:: Sound Editing

:: Music

:: Final Sound Mix

:: Color Correction/Grading

:: Raising Finishing Funds

:: Indie Post Legal Checklist

If you're like most micro-budget filmmakers, you likely blew your wad on production and will enter into post with very little to work with as far as a budget goes. The end of this section will cover your options as far as further fundraising goes, but in the meantime you will need to learn to find creative (i.e. free) solutions to your problems. Doing so will not only stretch the dollars that remain, but it's in every equity stakeholder's best interest to avoid taking on more further investment – every dollar an investor gives you is a dollar that'll need to be recouped and paid back before the film starts to turn a profit. Dollars are not easy to come by at this level, so if you ever want to see a fiscal payoff to all the work you'll have put into the project by its completion, you should be trying to minimize expenditures even if the funds are available. The one advantage you have going for you in post is that the time crunch you were subject to in production dissipates, which affords you the luxury of taking the time to ensure some quality to the work done despite your never-ending financial constraints.

One very comforting truth to be aware of, at least if you're operating in a major city with a sizeable enough pool of aspiring film industry workers, is that **ANYTHING** can be found and accomplished at little to no cost if you search and haggle long enough. The trick is to learn the delicate balance of portraying the production as a poor, struggling artistic pursuit one would feel compassionate enough towards to help out, but still will result in an end product that everyone involved will be proud to champion as a resume piece. Learning how to paint that picture, and portraying yourself as a worthy representative of it, is no small feat. This is particularly so over the medium of Craigslist, the most accessible way of finding low/no-cost post-production personnel, but one that most all job seekers approach with a heavy-handed wariness. Our specific solutions during each phase of post went as follows.

:: Rough Picture Assembly

If you were able to get an editor on set, or had one built into another crew member as we did for AGC, you should have this behind you already, for the most part. If not, it's the first step in sorting out all the ones and zeros you piled up during the shoot. It's best to let the editor work on his or her own, whether they are the director or not, to get to square one on the picture edit. They should have been chosen for the role because you trusted their eye in the first place, and the roughest of rough cuts is an instance where you should trust that.

:: Re-Shoots

When you sit down to watch the first cut, if you don't have a number of holes in the narrative you're either blessed with a brilliant director or an overwhelming abundance of luck. For the rest of us, some additional shooting will be in order. There were things we needed to reshoot and get better coverage on, particularly from the coffee shop location, as well as things we simply didn't realize the need for until we sat down and watched the footage we had cut together. We scheduled two days of shooting in early June, 2010, scratched together a skeleton crew, and negotiated a bargain basement hourly reshoot rate at the coffee shop in exchange for ordering dinner there. That went down as outlined in the following schedule that Matt put together, quoted verbatim:

:: DAY ONE – Sunset: 8:14 PM

:: Battery Park, North side of the fort

Call: 6:00 PM – TAKE LUNCH ORDER

Actors: Jessica Kaye

Shots: Delia walking around, Delia celebrating new job

Costumes: Interview outfit, add jacket/walk-around

outfit (striped scarf, red hoodie, blue sweater, skinny jeans)

Hair: Hair in a bun/hair down and curly

Props: None

:: Café One

Call: 9:00 PM – Lunch at 9 PM at Café One

Actors: Josh Folan, Jessica Kaye

Shots: Jon enters coffee shop, Delia typing, Establishing shot at coffee shop, Delia's coverage in hipster scene, Jon making coffee while Delia's on the phone, Delia outside on phone, Delia entrance coverage, Entire 3rd coffee shop scene, Jon closing coffee shop gate

Costumes: Jon's coffee shop uniform, Delia #1, Delia #2, Delia #3

Props: Computer, phone

:: Nook (Around corner from café)

Call: 12 AM

Actors: Josh Folan, Jessica Kaye

Shots: "What do we do now" scene

Costumes: Jon exterior, Delia #3

Props: None

:: Train

Call: 1 AM

Actors: Josh Folan, Jessica Kaye

Shots: Jon sitting alone, Delia sitting alone, Slow zoom

out from couple, Jon looking at Delia, Delia looking at Jon

Costumes: Jon exterior, Delia #3

Props: Cigarettes

:: DAY TWO – Sunset: 8:15 PM

:: Jon's Apartment

Call: 11:00 AM

Actors: Josh Folan

Shots: Jon getting dressed, Jon inspecting his face in mirror, Jon setting table, Jon opening closet, Jon MCU in Athena kill scene, Blood running down tub drain

Costumes: Jon dinner date, Jon white T

Props: Dinner setup, iPhone (remind Ryan), blood

:: Production Office

Call: 1 PM

Actors: Josh Folan

Shots: Jon leaving apartment for day

Costumes: Jon exterior

Props: None

JON WRAPPED

:: Maitlin Bathroom (Matt's Apt)

Call: 1:30 PM

Actors: Tiffany Lee

Shots: Lydia prepares bath, reaction shots in mirror, leaves Delia voicemail

Costumes: Robe

Props: phone

LYDIA WRAPPED

:: Delia's Apartment (Matt's Apt)

Call: 2:30 PM

Actors: Jessica Kaye

Shots: Delia getting her apartment keys from landlord (Frank cameo!)

Costumes: Delia #1

Props: Keys

:: Penn Station Exterior

Call: 5:30 PM

Actors: Jessica Kaye

Shots: Delia arriving in NYC, buying a hot dog

Costumes: Delia #1

:: Hotel Bathroom (Network Bathroom)

Call: 6:30 PM

Actors: Jessica Kaye

Shots: Delia applies makeup, Delia looks at pic of Lydia, Delia taking off makeup, Delia throwing hooker clothes away

Costumes: Hooker outfit

Props: Makeup

There were also a number of B-roll exteriors that Frank had to get, as well as some nighttime stuff down in Riverbank Park of me walking around. Because the HVX-200 we shot the bulk of the film on doesn't handle low-light situations very well and we couldn't afford to properly light the park this time around, we hired Saro Varjabedian and his Canon 5D for an evening to shoot the latter. Watching the beautiful footage Saro shot, the most notable of which is the park-walking montage in act one of the film, I was a little peeved we hadn't shot the entire film on his camera.

:: Picture Lock

In the logical flow chart for a feature film's post-production process, a definitive picture lock is an absolute must before moving into the sound editing phase. We were not aware of how detrimental ignoring this necessity would be to the sound edit, and would pay the price of that oversight many times over before finishing the film – particularly Ryan, who over time became our de facto supervising sound editor. Even the most minute picture changes – a frame or two – will result in sound not matching up with picture all over your editing timeline...a notion that in hindsight is so common sense it's sickening. DO NOT make the same mistake. Lock your picture edit, with unabated certainty, before starting in on sound. No blank slugs as "placeholders" for things you're convinced will be a certain length or any other tentative uncertainties. Lock it, no exceptions.

:: Sound Editing

This would prove to be the most troublesome area of the entire filmmaking process for us, by far. We had originally come to an agreement with our production mixer/recordist to handle the foley artistry, ambient sound, and dialogue mixing responsibilities in post in exchange for some contingency compensation on top of the (sizeable, relative to the fees anyone else made on the film) day rate he received for production days. To this day, I'm not sure if it was because of a lack of desire, or an inability, to do the job, but ultimately he would string us along for months beyond the generous delivery dates we set for him. There was even an instance where he claimed the hard drives were in the mail, and then as days past beyond his delivery date quotes, he made up a stories about them having been returned (he said he was drunk when he sent it), then later something about them being in the safe at his mom's house...very flakey stuff. When we finally did receive them the work was inadequate and incomplete, even by underfunded inexperience standards, a testament to the importance of checking references and **relevant** work history on a crew candidate before putting your future in their hands. The end result was us having to start from square one on the sound editing in November – four months after having locked the picture.

We turned to Craigslist to fill the newfound audio void. There was literally no money left in the budget at this point (we had yet to conduct our Indiegogo campaign) so we had little to offer candidates other than profit participation and a nominal, out-of-pocket stipend. The four of us decided it would be best to spread the responsibilities across three people – a foley artist, an ambient sound mixer, and a dialogue mixer. It seemed like a safer bet in case our nominal compensation led to one of them flaking on us, as well as better for our timeline with January festival deadlines looming. Ultimately one did flake, and the two guys that stuck with us shouldered the additional workload, above and beyond what they originally agreed to, like champions. Selfless, team-oriented work ethic like that is something you need to recognize and reward by pushing them to the top of your rolodex for similar work in the future, and both Adam Finley and Will Whatley – the guys that handled that stuff for us – are absolutely at the top of mine. We had their work back by mid December, and from there Ryan did the final polishing.

> **Poor Man's Film School Sidebar:** There are scenes in AGC where characters are shown watching a form of media; Jon and Delia are in a movie theater at one point, and the television is always on in the Maitlin household, which posed the question of what to choose for the content being watched in those scenarios. Neither would actually be seen by our audience, but audio would still need to be settled on. With the Maitlin household television, we added a laugh track to audio from the web series we had produced the year prior, *Bad Apples* (www.youtube.com/playlist?list=PLE91F94B266A47110), and laid it into the background with a hollow, old-school *The Benny Hill Show* feel to it. Old television shows with absurd laugh tracks are creepy, and creepy and unsettling is how we wanted the scenes in that house to come off. It is also a great little Easter egg for us. For the movie theater scene, we thought it made sense that these two disturbed characters would be inclined to go see something as equally unsettling as their own psyches. I had recently gotten wind that George Romero's

classic *Night of the Living Dead* had mistakenly slipped into the public domain years ago because of some sort of legal oversight on the copyright holder's behalf, so we used audio from that. Side-side lesson: don't ever let the rights to your film end up in the public domain. One look at the long list of vulture distributors on NotLD's IMDb Pro page should be all the motivation you need to never let anyone else exploit your hard work without having to compensate you for it.

:: Music

Wouldn't it be great to score your film with all the latest and greatest [insert despicable pop star #1 here] and [insert wretched pop star #2 here] songs that have headed up the uber-prestigious Billboard charts for the last six months? Well give up that dream, dreamer – the rights to those "songs" are expensive. Like, really expensive. I didn't even bother to research mainstream hits for *All God's Creatures* or *What Would Bear Do?*, but in budgeting more recent projects I've gotten quotes upwards of six figures for full worldwide usage in perpetuity. If you have that kind of money at your disposal, you don't need to worry about using the mindset I'm pitching you in this book. In fact, just go to the strip club and throw money in the air...you're going to be just fine.

Ok, if you're still reading then the spreadsheet cell containing the music allocation on your budget must be as barren as ours was, so I'll explain how we were able to procure each component of the AGC soundtrack (itunes.apple.com/us/album/all-gods-creatures/id544417636) – one of the components of the film I'm most proud of.

:: **Des Roar:** I woke up to a voicemail from a buddy one morning that he'd left, wasted, the night before outside a show he went to. We were still in pre, but he was aware of the subject matter and Des Roar has a track called "Ted Bundy Was a Ladies Man" that sounds as if it were written from scratch for our soundtrack, as well as entire LP (*Mad Things*) filled with dark, disturbing lyrics that embody both lead character's lives. He also used to bartend with the lead singer of the band, Ben Wolcott, at a place on the Lower East Side. We leveraged that connection for a meeting with the band after going to see them play at the Mercury Lounge on Houston, bought them a shot of Jame-O and laid out our interest. We negotiated a generous net profit participation deal with their manager and scored half our film in one fell swoop.

:: **Car Stereo Wars & Molotov Elysian:** Our music supervisor, Sherri Eldin, was a friend of Matt's that worked at a licensing and management company, Mother West. She brought a great online music database they have called "The Vault" to our attention, which we perused until we found a few tracks by these bands that were a great fit for the film. Charles Newman, the owner, amicably worked with us on a deferred compensation deal that hinged on net profits.

:: **Ajar:** A band that Sherri also knew. We negotiated a deal with them with no up-front cost to the film.

:: **The Dangerous Maybes:** Director Ryan Charles' brother is in the band. No work required.

:: **David Dabbon:** We eventually decided that some composed instrumentals would be necessary for the film, and David happened to be a friend of Ryan's that was willing to work with us for profit participation and his first feature film credit.

:: Final Sound Mix

The final mix is a very tough thing to accomplish at low/no cost, unless of course you have a personal connection willing to help you out. Without a proper professional studio facility and a knowledgeable sound technician to operate it, there's no way that I'm aware of to fine tune the audio to the specifications in the deliverables requirements of most distribution contracts – and those facilities and their operators are not cheap. Around the time the need arose for AGC, I had an ADR session come up for a film I had acted in, and I got to know the technician, Matt Craig, that ran them quite well by the end of that process. Talking with him about being up against the final mix for AGC, because he had never done so on a feature-length project (that all-important first feature credit poker chip, yet again), he was willing to talk discounted rates for the job. He was able to procure overnight sessions at an amazing facility he had a good relationship with at no cost, and he was very kind with the labor rates he asked of us. It took four long nights with him and Ryan in the studio to finish the mix, and one more with all four of us (Frank, Matt, Ryan and I) to go through it one final time.

Poor Man's Film School Sidebar: As great as Matt was to work with, and how great a job he did, we would later have an issue come up in the QC reporting where the music track "peaked" outside of the permitted ranges. We would come to learn that the music track needs to be set at a lower db level across the board in a film mix – something our technician had never encountered coming from a mostly music background. One of so many things you'd never learn until you actually make a film. Or read this book, I suppose.

A creative financing solution to not having the money for this is to have your audio editor get the sound mix to a point that is serviceable for festival exhibition and the like, and holding off on the final mix until an actual distribution deal is on the table, which is when a proper mix will be an absolute requisite. As long as your sound isn't a complete disaster to begin with, you can probably get by with your sound editor's best effort until there is definitely some money on the horizon.

:: Color Correction/Grading

Co-director Frank Licata had experience with color grading, so he was able to handle that responsibility at the commercial production facility one of our crew members worked at. A properly-calibrated color grading monitor is a necessity here – doing it at home on your Macbook Pro isn't going to cut it for a professional end product.

With *What Would Bear Do?* we didn't have the luxury of an "on-staff" colorist, so we would have to turn to craigslist and some serious bargaining to get three days of work out of Artificial Peach's DaVinci system.

:: Raising Finishing Funds

This likely will not be the last step in your post-production process, unless you are either very fortunate or very well funded – in which case you might just skip it, unless you need help covering distributor deliverables or festival costs. For most micro-budgeters, the money will run out during one of the previously covered steps in the process. For us, that step was just prior to the final sound mix stage. There are infinite ways to scratch together finishing funds – punking school kids out of their lunch money, risking sterility in paid medical studies, stealing from the tip jar at Starbucks – but your primary (and ethically viable) options here are:

> :: **Approaching existing/other investors for more capital.** This can be quite an uncomfortable conversation to have with people who are likely your friends and family, and who were skeptical whether you could actually make a profitable film to begin with. Convincing them that running out of money is not a sign of failure, and that giving you even more isn't a waste, will not be easy. You can also try to find new investors to bring into the fold, but unless you're willing to give up some of the filmmaker slice of the equity pie, the value of your existing

investors' stakes will change accordingly – the ownership pie never gets any bigger than 100%.

:: **Crowdfunding.** Putting together a campaign explaining what exact aspects of post you need financial help for, showing what you have accomplished to date in the form of trailers/teasers/excerpts, and being earnest about your goals for the film are the approaches to take with it. This is the route we went for AGC, and it brought in around $4000.

:: **Pay out of pocket.** Certainly the hardest option to swallow after having worked for free on a project for however long it took to get this far, but if you've exhausted all other means and want to see the film reach the finish line, that's the deal. We had to do a little of this as well, even with the successful crowdfunding campaign.

:: Indie Post Legal Checklist

:: Post crew deal memos. Don't get lazy just because you're in post - get a signed deal memo from anyone doing even the smallest of tasks, clearly defining what they are (or more likely are not) getting for their work and what time frame they'll be performing it in.

:: Depending on your need for and approach to finishing funds, you may need to rework your operating agreement to reflect a new ownership structure.

:: Music clearances. Any copyrighted music you use in the film will require all writers, performers and licensees for the songs to sign off on your usage. Get it in perpetuity, and for all media and exhibition forms – it's a cheap/easy alternative to obtain a license for festival use only, but you'll either have to rework the deal or remix your film to commercially exploit later on. That's a headache you don't want if a distribution offer does come along.

CUT TO:

Distribution (Or the Pursuit of It)

Distribution Checklist

:: Marketing Materials

:: Publicity

:: Niche Marketing

:: Event Marketing

:: Festival Strategy

:: Seeking Distribution & Approaching Film Markets

:: Distributor Negotiation & Delivery

:: Self-Distribution

:: Indie Distribution Legal Checklist

The order of the above steps isn't in any sort of chronological order, as the process of securing and/or conducting distribution is a convoluted one in most micro-budget scenarios. We started working on assembling our marketing materials, reaching out to reviewers and tapping into target niches long before we were in a position to profit from any interest we created. There are pros and cons to the creation of buzz prior to the monetization phase; a stockpiled audience (email list subscribers, Facebook and Twitter followers, etc.) can easily be accessed once the film is ready and that existing audience can be an interest beacon for traditional distributors, as well as a bargaining tool in your negotiations with them. On the other hand, an individual's interest in your film could very well never be as incentivized to buy as it is when they first become aware of it, so to not have the film available for sale at the brief moment you have someone's attention could result in lost sales. Given we endured the anguish of not really formulating one in advance, I strongly recommend you devise a well planned and advantageously timed marketing strategy that will allow you to make informed decisions...instead of the blind stabs we were taking for over a year prior to securing a distributor.

Unsure of our traditional distribution prospects, we decided to engage in some self-distribution around the time of our festival premier at the Hoboken International Film Festival in June of 2011 – which amounted to having a small run of DVDs printed up and sold from the website, as well as placing the film on the online VOD platform IndieFlix. Some distribution personnel would argue this course of action diminishes a title's attractiveness to a distributor, as they want to be able to direct the initial release of the film to their liking and hate the idea of having already missed sales when acquiring a title, but it ultimately did not prevent us from securing a deal. Osiris Entertainment did ask that we pull the DVD offer from the website and remove the film from any and all VOD platforms, but that was the extent of the "backlash." Based on that experience, I'd be hard pressed to come up with a reason to recommend against this type of "soft self-release" if you are in an open-ended distribution search with no potential A-list festival premieres on the horizon. With that distribution and marketing climate stated, I'll cover how we tackled each of these categories.

:: Marketing Materials

You'll have an endless need for content - teasers, trailers, promo videos, stills, etc. – so start stacking it all in a neat, organized little pile that you can quickly sift through when the need arises. Some critical tools will be covered here, but you should tirelessly be cooking up new, unique ways to spin the content you are able to compile in ways to help market the film.

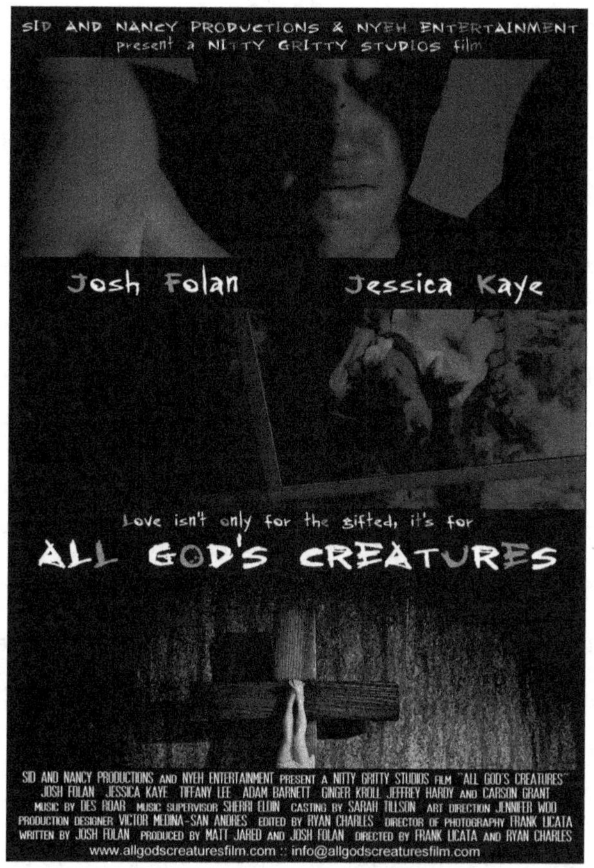

Original AGC Key Art

:: **Key Art.** I originally took some conceptual drafts we kicked around as key art possibilities and just went off on my own with Adobe Fireworks to put together the poster we would use until securing distribution, after which it was retooled by Osiris into the image currently in circulation. I used stills from John Harris, tracked down a cool font on the interwebs, and did what I could with my limited design proficiency. We were ever-so-proud of keying the word "LOVE" in red into the title of the film itself, as well as a few other little hidden messages in the production company text at the top. With WWBD, I turned to Craigslist and sought out a young artist, James Eads, to put together an illustration based off stills we had from the shoot – again, for his first feature film credit and a nominal stipend.

:: **Press Kit.** You should already have the groundwork laid for this by the distribution stage, so you'll just be updating and rounding out the existing document here. Update the bios of key cast and crew, include a page about the bands you've involved the music of, include a thoughtful note from the key filmmakers about what the film means to them, update the full cast and crew credit listing with post-production personnel, write a short background paragraph explaining all the trials and tributes that were weathered to make the film a reality, include any press coverage you were able to drum up during the shoot, and be sure to highlight anything else that makes your film unique/interesting/cool. Ultimately, the purpose of the document is to sell the film, so sell the goddamn film in the writing of it. You can pull up AGC's at www.allgodscreaturesfilm.com/wp-content/themes/aeg/AGCPressKit.pdf and WWBD's at www.whatwouldbeardofilm.com/WWBD_Press_Kit.pdf.

:: **Videos.** This is where you have to really get creative. The effectiveness of the promotional video content you create to market the film will hinge on whether you are able to encapsulate the best aspects of your film and convey them to a viewer in the short attention span you are likely to be afforded.

That means you need to pinpoint what is unique, interesting, captivating – whatever the selling point of your product is – and be able to fire it at the speed of light into the potential consumer's psyche in a fashion that leaves them hankering for more. In the case of AGC, we catered to the love story theme by creating 30-second matching his and hers teasers that touched on the troubled individual lives of the lovers. We were very aware of the micro-budget filmmaking aspect of our work, and didn't hesitate to highlight it in a short documentary interview series we shot with Tym Moss, one of the day player actors in the film, while talking with him for his internet radio show. We ended up naming the series *Shoot to Kill: The Making of All God's Creatures* – you can watch the full series at www.youtube.com/playlist?list=PLE43B9BE52B30C38B.

On WWBD, with the comedic subject matter in mind, I've cut similarly styled his and hers teasers that were of course a smattering of the funny moments between the guy and girl pairings in the lead foursome. I've also been using some of the better outtakes as short teasers.

You'll definitely need a full two to three minute traditional trailer, though I'd try to keep it much closer to the former. You'll likely have a natural inclination to try to tell the story here, as we struggled to defy with both films, but you have to resist that urge and keep in mind that this is a sales tool – so your goal is to sell the film, not tell the story told in it. What accomplishes that best is project-specific, but understand you don't need to follow any rules. If it's more interesting to put the something from the end of the film as the opening image of the trailer, where you should be setting up the characters and plot, then by all means put it there. Making two minutes of awesome that leaves the viewer telling his or her friend to google the trailer is the sole purpose here. The one counter to this theory is if you full-on mislead the consumer about what the film is about, you risk them reacting negatively when they watch the movie itself and trashing the film in their social circles because it wasn't their cup of tea – I've seen that happen a lot lately with art films being portrayed as something they're not to get asses in theater seats – Nicholas Winding Refn's *Drive* and Harmony Korine's *Spring Breakers* are examples of this. Things have worked out alright for both filmmakers in those cases, but then again they had Ryan Gosling and James Franco at their disposal.

:: Publicity

I tend to skew towards the overzealous side when it comes to my work, so I was out driving up interest – or attempting to, anyhow – on AGC long before we had a finished product to show anyone who might actually want to watch it. I was emailing hundreds of bloggers, critics and other press personnel with every outlet I could mine up at least a year before we completed all phases of post. While I always encourage being proactive, I definitely sparked interests that waned by the time I was able to get a respectable cut of the film in their hands. I'd suggest just waiting until the film is actually finished, seeing as you ideally would want to time any reviews or coverage with the release of the film. That desire is of course contingent on you having a means of releasing it, and if you are having a hard time securing a distributor getting some good reviews to lean on in your sales pitches to acquisitions personnel could be a reason to allow the reviewers to publish their feedback prior to the film being available for sale. There is also the possibility you've decided to release the film in some capacity on your own, in which case you should try to time coverage with that date. Whatever your needs may be, journalists/bloggers are very accustomed to the practice of timed releases in their coverage of films, so don't hesitate to ask.

The best way to track down and get a hold of the individuals that you'll want watching and talking about your film is probably Twitter, which anyone with anything to say these days is utilizing to disseminate their opinions to the masses. Finding one or two people who are worth pursuing the opinion of will lead to suggestions of similar reviewers, and you can spider your way to an endless supply of people who watch and critique films, and may be willing to take a look at yours. There are also a number of anal retentive individuals who have done the hard work for you already, having taken the time to make lists of press industry personnel within the Twitter framework. I am one of those individuals – you can pull up the larger of my two (the max number of accounts you can currently add to a single list is 500) such lists at www.twitter.com/joshfolan/film-press. You're welcome. Don't contact them through Twitter, as both messages and direct tweets from unknown accounts tend to be more of an annoyance that just get ignored amongst all the chatter that makes up social media, but rather take their name and press outlet they work for and start querying those keywords in hopes of tracking down a direct email address that you can send a polite and properly-written email to. The email should be brief, with the particulars of the film (title, logline, notable cast and crew, a couple choice existing press blurbs that speak highly of the film – if you've procured any – and links to the press kit PDF and your best teaser/trailer. No email attachments, that's bush league and the number one method of directing your email straight into the condescending quarantine of their junk filter. Ask if they'd be willing to take a look at the film when they have the time, not if they would review it for you; learn to ask for things without actually asking for them, it's less schleppy. If you're a filmmaker emailing them about a film, they already know you want it reviewed – so don't be a schmuck.

Should you be fortunate enough to get a reply, kindly thank them for their time and ask if they would prefer a digital screener (which should be your preferred method, it's cheaper) or a DVD in the mail, and keep note of all the interaction in your contacts. If you are not sending screeners out immediately upon request, keep a detailed list of people who are due a copy and make sure you deliver when you said you would, or send them a note near the date letting them know it's not quite ready and when it can be expected. After you've sent the screener, follow up every couple of weeks to check in and see if they've gotten a chance to check it out. Even the most obscure reviewers can have an overwhelming number of films to sift through, so try to keep yours in the to-do pile without being overbearing. The through line here is organization and communication – don't fuck them up…ever. You're already fighting an uphill battle to garner some attention because you and your micro-budget film are irrelevant in the industry and public eye, don't sabotage yourself further by being a discombobulated, fuck-up artist.

:: Niche Marketing

Niche marketing isn't any different in broad protocol than the traditional variety; identify your market, research and assess the ideal method of reaching it, execute that reach in as clever and attention-gathering a way as you can concoct. The big difference between niche and mainstream marketing is the scale of the returns your efforts result in. Your average studio project operates with a corporate mentality – everything is geared across the board to minimize costs and maximize gains, and they do this by trying to produce product with mass appeal (star actors, using brands with widespread public awareness already built into them, etc.) already, and then saturating every conceivable media outlet in the known universe with advertisements of the coming soon content their research has shown is eagerly awaited by the public for consumption. Basically, they want you to subconsciously think that you'd have to be an asshole to not go buy a ticket. That sort of shotgun approach is neither possible nor appropriate for a tiny film with no A-list actors or comic book superhero subject matter to lean on, which means you'll have to rely on attracting and engaging small, specialized audiences if you want your film to be seen.

There's more than one school of thought as to how to identify and approach groups that your particular film would appeal to, but ultimately they all boil down to achieving a clear-cut understanding of what the core of your film amounts to...not always as easy as it might seem. This far into the process, you likely have a very detached POV towards the film and would be well served to at least listen to some trusted outside opinions, so I recommend showing an edit to those trusted opinion factories and picking their brain a bit about what they see as the core themes and subject matter of your story. We saw *All God's Creatures* as a love story between two dark souls, so we targeted groups that might have an interest in the parts of the character's lives they held close to the vest – prostitution with Delia and murder with Jon. Some specific ideas we had:

:: **Craigslist Personal Ads.** Posting mock craigslist ads in the personals section, vaguely implying we were a working girl offering up her services. We set up auto-replies on a fake email account that emailed back with an in-character suggestion to check out the film, including an embedded teaser with sexually provocative content. If morally questionable tactics like this don't sit well with you, you're probably in the wrong industry.

:: **Serial Killer Blogs.** Some intense googling turned up an endless supply of small internet-based communities composed of people with an affinity for anything and everything serial killer-related. We stalked the point man for each and tried to work mention of the film into their community in any way they were open to.

In hindsight, this is one worthwhile area where we could have done more to promote the film. A lot of our efforts here were exerted when we were self-distributing, long before the title was available on a visibly commercial level, and they would have likely been much more impactful if they had took place once the film had been released into larger retailers, or (a more proactive idea) conducted a second time after the fact.

MISSING

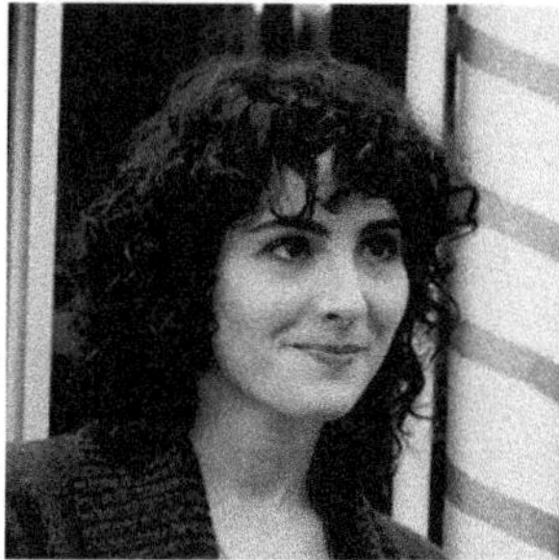

DELIA MAITLIN

AGE: 24
EYES: BROWN
HAIR: BLACK
HEIGHT: 5'6"
WEIGHT: 115 LBS.

LAST SEEN AT A COFFEE SHOP ON 145TH & AMSTERDAM AVE IN MANHATTAN

DELIA MAITLIN, RECENTLY RELOCATED TO NEW YORK FROM PHILADELPHIA, WAS LAST SEEN FREQUENTING A COFFEE SHOP ON MANHATTAN'S UPPER WEST SIDE ON MARCH 26TH, 2010.

PLEASE HELP

IF YOU HAVE ANY INFORMATION ABOUT DELIA'S WHEREABOUTS OR WOULD LIKE TO KNOW MORE ABOUT THE FEATURE FILM ALL GOD'S CREATURES, PLEASE VISIT

WWW.ALLGODSCREATURESFILM.COM

A mock missing poster for Delia

:: Event Marketing

Without the proper money in place to promote them, live events (particularly screenings) are easily one of the most labor-intensive ways of getting your film out there. As is the case with most difficult things in life though, the hard work spent on them can also have some of the highest fiscal and promotional payoff of any potential marketing efforts you might make with a low-budget project. I'll touch on how we were able to get the film in front of live audiences and some of the ways we handled maximizing the gain from doing so.

The screening alone can be a tough thing to procure, let alone organizing something worthwhile around it. Most theater venues, even the smaller art house options (Cinema Village near Union Square in NYC, just to give an example of the scope I'm talking) have a requisite P&A spend just to book a film for any run at all. Amounts here are situational and negotiable, and you might even be able to convince a theater booker to waive it altogether if they happen to have an opening on their schedule they are afraid of not being able to fill, so if you're pinching pennies don't be afraid to say you can't swing a spend and need to work out a time when that's not going to be necessary. As long as you understand you probably are not going to get the most ideal showing nights and times, and that they will have little choice in replacing you with another film that has better odds of tallying more dependable box office dollars, you can find somewhere to screen your film with enough due diligence.

Festivals are of course the ideal alternative to hosting your own screenings – the marketing is done for you, they have an existing audience base they draw off of to drive people into seats, and press relations are also their responsibility. In short, they do a lot of leg work for you, and that allows for all the exhausting effort you would put into just scratching the surface of marketing potential on your own to become a stress-free added bonus. Assuming you don't get a seat at the big boy table, utilizing the smaller festivals as a means of hosting test screenings and/or cast and crew screenings is a great solution. NewFilmmakers New York, which operates out of the Anthology Film Archives in the East Village, is a great example of this. They operate as a film festival does, accepting submissions through Withoutabox for around $50, with two major differences – they accept submissions and screen films year round, and while I don't want to say they accept pretty much everything, they accept pretty much everything. You're not getting any box office control, or any say in what shorts your invitees will have to sit through before your film, but a guaranteed screening that you can invite your cast and crew to for nothing more than that $50 outlay and the cost of their tickets is a fairly reasonable expenditure.

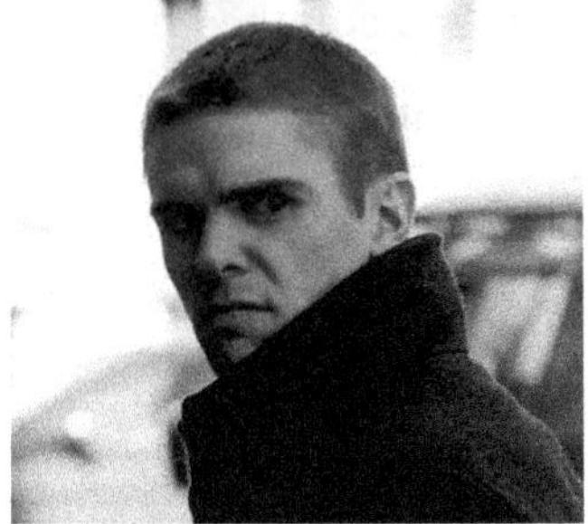

A mock wanted poster for Jon

There are also a number of alternative screening venue solutions out there as well. Upscale hotels, the Tribeca Grand in NYC for example, have nice screening rooms that I've seen friends procure for nothing more than organizing a cash bar gathering in the hotel's lounge on a weeknight prior to the showing of the film. Some lounges and nightclubs have the equipment and setup necessary for it, and are happy to organize something on an off-peak volume night that lures bodies in the door to buy a few drinks. As repeated time and time again in this writing, creativity (and an aggressive emailing mentality) is the key to cost-effective exhibition solutions.

However you organize the screening, you need to concoct a clever way to market it or your labor of love will be screening in front of a room full of empty seats. Infusing your campaign with the style and feel of your film, and spinning that into something you're able to engage a group of people with is a challenge with a truly infinite number of variables, and this book is supposed to be a case study, so instead of trying to provide some sort of a vague approach outline I'll just explain the "All God's Creatures Body Count" bar crawl and scavenger hunt contest we staged for our cast and crew screening in the NewFilmmakers Series on May 25th, 2011.

Body Count contest placard

The basic premise of *Body Count* was that Jon, the main character, was a serial killer, and we would create "bodies" to stash in a number of bars around the screening venue and up 2nd Avenue in advance of the night of the event. Each "body" was a large laminated placard that looked like the one pictured above, hidden in a not-so-secret place in the venue, each one representing a different victim of Jon's. We used the character names in the film itself, as well as some additional we made up specifically for the contest. Each placard had a QR code that linked to a specific confirmation web page we had in place on our web server that the finder of the body was supposed to show the bartender in the venue the night of the event for a pre-ordained drink deal of some sort. The actual image above was the general flier we wallpapered Manhattan's Lower East Side with leading up to the event, which directed people to the contest's web-based explanation at www.allgodscreaturesfilm.com/bodycount. We incentivized participation by offering small prizes for collecting a certain number of bodies (represented by the unique confirmation numbers on each body's web page), and sold bar managers on the idea by explaining that for simply offering a drink deal on the night in question and letting us tape up the placard somewhere in the bar for a week, we would guarantee them some business. We listed the participating venues on the information web page, and then wrote some thinly-veiled clues for each venue to direct people to where the placard was located within, and all the elements were in place at no cost to us other than the placard and flier printing – which I convinced my girlfriend to have printed and laminated for us at her office at a cost of no cost.

The night of the screening will be a chaotic whirlwind regardless of how well organized you are, so mentally prepare accordingly. Tech snafus will inevitably take place (our sound had some issues, which were expected but excruciating nonetheless – for us that is, few others cared or noticed) and things will get off schedule, but do all you can to savor all your hard work being enjoyed by an actual audience. Things you should absolutely do at every event: gather email addresses, sell DVDs and anything else you're monetizing the project with, and GET FEEDBACK. Draw up an original and anonymous questionnaire that encourages engagement, but isn't so vaguely-phrased that it confuses people even more about your weird indie movie. Hand it out with a program as people enter the theater and you thank them for coming, and then have a drop box (and a number of writing utensils) conveniently stationed outside the theater doors.

:: Festival Strategy

There's more to festival strategy than blindly dumping your film into the Sundance hat on Withoutabox and patiently waiting for your impersonal rejection letter months later. Once you emotionally cope with not playing ball on the big league festival circuit, should that fate transpire, quite a few nice exhibition opportunities still remain out there peppered amongst the vast wasteland of festivals existing with little purpose beyond siphoning cash from publicity-starved independent filmmakers' pockets. A little googling goes a long way when trying to separate the men from the boys in the festival realm. From there you'll want to single out festivals with agendas that align with or have a physical proximity to the themes and/or subject matter in your film, upping your chances of being programmed and thereby making the money spent on the submission process a little more worthwhile from an aggregate standpoint. Was your film shot in the desert? The Phoenix festival is well done, and their programmers clearly don't mind deserts. Have a gritty New York film? There's a ton of smaller neighborhood festivals in NYC that will give you an opportunity to drive some press up in a major market if you're accepted. Ultimately, understand that selection committees are just a grouping of opinions, not an omnipotent collection of film gods – appeal to their sensibilities, and you just might make the cut.

> **Poor Man's Film School Sidebar:** Include a cover letter with your submission. Surprisingly few filmmakers take this opportunity to separate their submission from the pack with an eloquently-scribed love letter about their baby and all the hard work that went into it.

:: Seeking Distribution & Approaching Film Markets

Effect:

All God's Creatures, with no "stars", created by "unknown" filmmakers, and produced with less than $25k to work with is picked up for distribution in late 2011. By May 2012 it can be purchased through the biggest retailer in the known universe (Walmart) and numerous other retail outlets.

Cause:

:: **Make a movie.** Preferably a good one with a unique and interesting story, compelling characters, and a few commercial sales tools (sex, nudity, gore, comedy, super heroes – that sort of thing).

Seems an obvious step, yet it is quite often overlooked. Particularly the "good" part. I hear inexperienced producer say things akin to "it's a so-so horror script, but I just want to get a feature made" with alarming frequency, and it's no surprise at all how much unwatchable schlock ends up getting made as a result of that lackluster intention. If you don't have something unique about your film to passionately pitch to distributors when you finally get a few to listen to you, why the hell would they invest their time and money trying to create an audience for it?

:: **Formulate a pitch.** An airtight one that doesn't sound like anything you've read anywhere else, and DEFINITELY not any of that "Terminator meets Christmas Vacation" shit. If you get an acquisitions executive on the phone and you sputter out one of those for your little movie - that does not have a Schwarzenegger, Chevy Chase, or even an Uncle Eddie - it will be the last time you speak with that particular individual. My pitch with AGC was that "it boiled down to a dark, twisted love story between these two really fucked up people – a serial killer and a prostitute. And while a story like this would typically zero in on those elements, the killing and the sex, ours aims to make those things ancillary because of the focus on the love story." Yes, you will get very sick of hearing yourself repeat your airtight pitch...over and over and over and over. And over. And...over. That is, if you do the amount of legwork that will be required to actually convince a distribution professional that investing in your little film is worthwhile.

:: **Make a pretty PDF.** A press kit. These days this means an EPK (Electronic Press Kit), of which your pretty PDF will be a part of. The EPK will contain the numerous clever/mysterious/hilarious teasers and trailers that you have created to market your film with, your jaw-dropping original key art, any press interview video clips you had the foresight to arrange while filming the movie, any press clippings/screenshots that pertain to the film, the countless production stills, as well as the press kit PDF itself. Try to streamline all your marketing tools with the same look and feel – brand awareness and recognition is marketing 101. If you don't have an eye for making these things look professional, find someone who does and chain them in your basement until they agree to do it for you.

:: **You have your sales kit now - what the hell do you do with it, right?** The first step in selling anything is identifying who the most appropriate buyers are. In this case, they are film distributors and believe it or not, they are starving for good product. Contrary to popular belief, they do not spend their days waiting by their phones and email inboxes for the next opportunity to shit on the hopes and dreams of the poor, unknown filmmaker. They pray every waking moment for a call from a well-spoken, well-rounded human being who can conversationally explain why their film will be able to make both the distributor and the filmmaker a dump truck of money, and who won't drive the distributor bonkers with artistically-driven melodrama over the next ten years (a typical length of a distribution deal). So be that girl or guy. That's step one in the actual sales process - understand they want and need what you have, you just have to present it like a sane human being with an air of professionalism to get them to listen.

:: **On to identifying those buyers.** I'm going to assume you didn't get into Sundance, Cannes, Tribeca, or even SXSW. If you did, you're gifted and/or lucky and you don't need to read filmmaking advice written by me. Good for you. For the rest of us, you can likely cross the household (at least in my household) name and studio distributors off your list - Focus Features, the Weinstein Company, etc. They deal in "big" films and if you're not a big enough fish with an amazing enough product to get into any of those aforementioned festivals, they probably are not buying what you're selling. The answer for us "small" filmmakers is the American Film Market (AFM), held in Santa Monica every winter. It costs a few hundred bucks for a pass for the second half of the market, which is about the time when the distributors have finished the bulk of the selling of their existing catalogue, their primary purpose for being there, and are willing to talk acquisitions. On top of the selling opportunity being in attendance presents, it also pulls the curtain back and exposes the wizard that is the mysterious distribution industry as seen by the indie filmmaker – it's a hell of a learning experience and networking opportunity even if you fail to sell your movie. Once you sign up, you will have access to a listing of every single company that will be at the market - the keys to daddy's convertible, so hurry up and wrap this thing around a telephone pole before he changes his mind. You take that list and you pull up your IMDb Pro subscription and dissect each and every one of them; the types of films they deal in (genre, budget range, "star power"), how many they take on a year, all the personnel that have "acquisitions" in their job title. You dump all that into a spreadsheet and start identifying the companies that are matches based on those genre and budget range variables. Put it a little star next to the ones that match up with your film - these are your targets.

:: **Pick up the phone and call them.** Start with the person with the job title, of those with "acquisitions" in them, that sounds the most important. Often this means having a "VP" designation in there somewhere. Call their office. Be put on hold for ten minutes, then transferred to a general voicemail box that isn't for the specific person you asked for. Leave a friendly message with your pitch and contact info, and that you will be in attendance at AFM and would love to set up a short meeting on Sunday, Monday, or Tuesday (Wednesday is a wash at the market, everyone is clearing out by then) of that second week. Hang up and send an email explaining all those same things, and that you'll try them again in a few days. Wash, rinse, repeat. Do this for every single company that makes sense as a buyer. Keep track on your spreadsheet of when you last spoke to the person, when you said you'd be in touch again for follow up, and when and to whom you're redirected when you find out you're hunting down the wrong person. And if you secure a meeting, for God's sake write it down and keep it.

:: **Do your homework.** So you've got a meeting, or a request for a screener, or even just an expression of positive interest from one of your target distributors. Now you need to find out whether or not this company you're so excited about has a track record of keeping their promises and making good on their financial obligations to filmmakers, and the only way to do that is to ask the filmmakers they're currently working with whether or not that is the case. Back to IMDb Pro, where you'll look up the producers, or often the director/producer multi-hyphenate in the case of smaller films, of the titles the company has listed as having distributed. Shoot these filmmakers a cordial email asking about their experience to date with the company, and most are happy to give their insight – some will even talk your ear off about it. Do that with a range of titles in the distributor's catalogue; some from recently, some from a few years back that have experienced the full distribution cycle with the company. Not every filmmaker is going to be ecstatic about their experience, so take any one opinion with a grain of salt, but if you're hearing bad things from three, four, five people it's quite likely you'd end up having less-than-stellar feedback if you took a deal with them and were asked the same question down the line. Expect to be doing this same thing with any prospect that presents itself throughout your distribution pursuit.

:: **Work the AFM.** You've mailed out a ton of screeners and those pretty PDFs to eager distribution reps with all the companies you targeted, you've got a few meetings set up, your Starbucks gold card is all charged up (that last preparation tactic is moot, the closest chain coffee store to the Loews Hotel is a Coffee Bean) and you're ready to sell your ass off. Now what the hell is the AFM, exactly? It's basically a hotel lobby on entertainment business steroids. You walk in and Variety jams three copies of their daily AFM-edition rag in your face, so you can read all about the millions of dollars that some film with one of those goddamn twilight kids attached to it was just financed with yesterday, then some guy dressed in an oversized foam space suit tries to tell you all about Troma Entertainment's latest Sci-Fi title (note to self: don't market my films like that...ever), and you can't find that bathroom. It's to the left of the doors when you first walk in the hotel – just follow that yahoo screaming into his Bluetooth earpiece. The line is backed up all the way past the information desk though. While you're waiting in line, get out the most updated map of the company booth locations you can get your hands on and start plotting your trajectory through the hotel. Start with the companies that directly invited you to come speak with them at the market, and work your way down through the companies that said you don't have a snowball's chance in hell of getting a moment of their attention because they'll be too busy selling the amazing product in their existing catalogue. The "booths" are not booths at all, they're actual hotel rooms than have been converted into office suites just for these purposes. The doors are open, or will be at some point, so just walk in and ask to speak to the acquisitions representative you already know for a fact is in attendance (because you already did your homework), and if they're not in ask if you can schedule an appointment with them or when they'll be available to speak. If they're not available at all, ask if you can leave a screener and hard copy of your press kit, which you should have plenty of.

:: **Most important of all this is the follow up.** You are not Harvey Weinstein, so it's very unlikely you're going to initiate a bidding war at the market and sign a deal that will be announced in one of those AFM Variety issues. So keep good notes after every meeting. Know when you're supposed to follow up after the market and do so. Send your pretty PDFs and screeners to the people that request them. Call them just frequently enough to not completely annoy them, but understand that they understand – they're in sales too. Sales is about persistence, so be persistent. In the words of Derek Connolly, channeled through Mark Duplass in *Safety Not Guaranteed* (sidebar: see that movie if you haven't already), "There's no sense in nonsense when the heat is hot."

:: Distributor Negotiation & Delivery

So all the blood, sweat and tears that have went into making this film of yours has just careened into the brick wall of an offer for a distribution deal? That's it! We've done it! The Holy Grail of a small independent film is within our grasp! Get my mom on the phone while I pick out what shade of laser red Lamborghini I'm gonna buy, where do I sign?!?!

Hold your horses, cowboy. A PDF contract in your inbox that you don't really understand is no reason to get mom on the horn. Assuming you've already done your homework and you know whether the company is worth their salt based on an aggregate opinion of filmmakers they have worked with, past and present, there are still a number of factors that need to be weighed and negotiated before jumping on board with a distributor. Major deal points you need to be concerned with at this level are listed below, and by "this level" I mean you need to understand a micro-budget feature with no large talent draw has virtually no profit potential in a theatrical release, and that the old filmmaker adage that theatrical play will drive ancillary sales is also a pipe dream. We're talking DVD, television and VOD dollars here, you dreamer, you.

:: **Term.** The low side you'll likely find here is seven years, standards fall anywhere in between there and ten years, and perpetuity is not out of the question. Whatever the length you settle on, understand it's going to be a long time and that you will have to work with this company (barring their bankruptcy – not uncommon in the distribution industry) and, more importantly, the people running it for the life of the contract. Tensions tend to arise in even the best of filmmaker-distributor dynamics, so if you don't like who you're dealing with from the get-go, you'll really hate them when all that red starts rolling in on those quarterly statements.

:: **Territory.** The world is divided up into a slew of distribution territories, and you don't necessarily need to sign them all away on any one deal. The most simplistic of divisions on a US deal is domestic and foreign, the combined of which is termed worldwide. What's appropriate for you and your film is dependent on your situation. If your film, for any number of potential reasons (cast, producer relationships, subject matter), has strong prospects in a particular territory, it might be wise to negotiate that out of a worldwide deal offer. If the company you're dealing with doesn't seem to have much global reach, maybe you should only be discussing domestic terms – vice versa if their acumen lies in foreign sales. As with everything, your strategy here is only as sound as the research you do.

:: **Format.** Rights can also be broken up into the various mediums of distribution – DVD, television, television VOD, digital VOD, merchandising, and any other mode of monetization that can be dreamt up. The toughest one to accurately value here is digital VOD, which is completely wide-open territory at present. I also feel a lot of smaller distributors are still of an old school mindset that doesn't pay much attention to this profit sector. If you can hold onto these rights for your own private exploitation, or to repurpose them with someone who specializes in the field, I'd recommend you do so.

:: **Marketing Expenses.** These are the recoupable dollars the distributor can spend (without additional filmmaker approval) before the filmmaker starts seeing their share of profits; A.K.A. the reason many a filmmaker never sees a back-end dime out of their distribution deal. On the founded side, these are the expenses the distributor incurs while out selling your film to buyers – screeners, one sheets, posters, film market booths/rooms, travel attributed to your film's sales, etc. The gray area here is that a distributor has a vast catalogue of films they are selling at any one time, so if your distributor takes their 12-film catalogue to a market and their room there costs $12k, it should incur a $1000 charge against your film's sales, no? Well, what if the market is Berlin and it's a known fact your film is not of interest to the buyers your distributor will be talking to, and the sales results for your film reflect that at the close of said market? Should your title be charged the same figure as those that were passionately pushed? Arguable either way really, and these accounting appropriations come up a lot in a distributor's normal business practice. It is imperative that you have the marketing expenses cap in your contract defined at a reasonable level. Standards here are all over the place, $25-100k, but for a small title there isn't much reason to allow this to balloon past $40k. Keep it as low as possible, as there is always the option of granting approval for going above and beyond the figure for a viable reason.

:: **Revenue Share.** The overall profit split between the filmmaker and distributor, after expenses are deducted. You'll see a lot of 50-50 offers here, all of which are unreasonable and an attempt to take advantage of the business inexperience many distributors expect filmmakers to suffer from. You should be aiming for 25/75 to 35/65%, in your favor.

:: **Cash Advance.** The biggy. This is the sum you receive just for signing the contract and delivering the film in accordance with it. It is not an easy thing to convince a distributor to ante up at this budget tier. A company offering up-front cash wants to see some assurance that the film will have returns that make that outlay worthwhile – and there isn't much in the way of assurance about a film with no marquee talent on the poster. This is also very often the only money a filmmaker ever sees from their distribution deal, hence it being such a sought after deal point. There is no such thing as a standard here, but understand that it is recoupable – so whatever they give up here will come off the top of revenues as they start to come in, as long as those revenues are in fact collected. What that means is if they're not offering up an advance of any kind then they have assumed no risk on this joint venture you are supposedly partnering with them for, which isn't much of a vote of confidence in that venture. A distributor with no cash outlay can basically toss your film against the wall to see if it sticks – great if it does, if it doesn't then onto the next title. If a company isn't willing to offer up something here, you have to question their commitment to really going all out in selling your film. Also to be weighed is the fact it will cost you money to fulfill a distribution deal. At the bare minimum, you can expect to spend $1000 for a letter of opinion from a lawyer about your film's clearances, $3000-4000 on errors and omissions insurance, and anywhere from $500-2000 on deliverable formats and QC reporting (assuming your film does not need any serious video or sound correction to meet those QC expectations). With no advance on the table, you have to ask yourself if it may end up costing you money in the long run, should creative accounting never show any profits for the filmmaker side of the revenue split. Even if there is an advance, you should be aware that the bulk of it will likely not be in your hands until well AFTER all these delivery expenses are incurred.

:: **Deliverable Requirements.** None of the research I did before working out the deal on *All God's Creatures* made any mention of this being something you should concern yourself with in the negotiations, but after my experience I would absolutely recommend you talk about paring these down from what are no doubt above and beyond the necessary delivery formats for your film. We had an HD film, as most any is these days, yet our contract required that we deliver 16x9 and 4x3 versions in both NTSC and PAL formats, on digital betacam tapes (a standard definition format) and HDCAM. Additionally, we had to provide an uncompressed Apple ProRes 422 digital file on a hard drive. Each one of the tapes needed to have a QC report conducted on them by a reputable third party post production house, which runs upwards of a $100 per report. While I'm not blaming the distributor entirely for our difficulties in delivery – we had a very hard time procuring a lot of this stuff because of inexperience and lack of funding – they ultimately only needed that ProRes. All the tape-based stuff we dealt with turned out to be a complete waste of time and money, and on my next deal I will absolutely steer the ship towards only having to deliver that medium.

:: **Distribution Deal Profit Formula.** Let's say you secure a deal where the terms are a 65-35 revenue split, in favor of the filmmaker, with a $40k marketing expense cap and a $25k advance. You get your full $25k within 45 days of the street (release) date of the film. For the sake of simplicity, we'll say your distributor accounts on an annual basis (though quarterly is the least frequent accounting method you should be tolerant of in an actual deal), and the annual statement you get a month after the one year anniversary reports that they did $65k in sales, and spent $22k on marketing.

So, Sales – Distributor Revenue Split – Expenses – Advance = Filmmaker Revenue

:: ex. 65,000 – (65,000*0.35) – 22,000 – 25,000 = -4750

So that means you still have $4750 left of your advance to pay back before you see a dime from the revenue share, and next year there will surely be more expenses to deduct before profits are split. Hopefully you see how things could never make it into the black on these deals.

Everything is negotiable; nothing in the deal is unable to be augmented. If you feel you or another company than the one you are working out a deal with is more suited to monetize an aspect of your film, fight to exclude those rights from the agreement. We felt we had assembled a particularly strong soundtrack for the film, and our distributor's track record didn't seem to imply that accompanying soundtrack marketing and sales were something they had dealt much with, so we asked to keep our soundtrack rights and they didn't have the slightest qualm with us doing so. Another company we were speaking to about distributing the film itself, Phase One Communications, had a strong music division, so we went back to them letting them know we were going another direction with the film but would like to work out a soundtrack deal – you can find it on iTunes at http://itunes.apple.com/us/album/all-gods-creatures/id544417636, an indicator of a mission accomplished.

A word on confidence in your ability to negotiate; the natural inclination, as the poor impoverished filmmaker, when a decent distribution deal finally comes down the pipe is that you are lucky to have it, and there were individuals in our brain trust on AGC that absolutely wanted to take whatever was presented to us. I fought tooth and nail to maximize the deal, increasing our advance and lowering our market expense cap from the initial offer. No rationale businessman is going to walk away from a deal just because you counteroffer – as long as it's a reasonable counter – so don't be afraid to ask for more if you feel it's warranted...or even if it's not, for that matter.

:: Self Distribution

A distributor not bestowing their all-knowing approval on you should by no means crush your hopes of people seeing your film – I was told of one picture that was picked up by a distributor, and later the producer/lead actor was told by the owner of the company that the reason he acquired the title was that his girlfriend thought that said actor was "hot." He relayed this information as he showed the producer/actor a picture of this all-to-Californian-blond on his phone, much in the same vein as an annoying mother hangs her child's terrible art class abomination on the fridge. The point here being acquisition decisions are made for a myriad of reasons, and those reasons seldom have anything to do with the film's artistic merit.

That said, self distribution is last on the list here because it's pretty close to the bottom of every filmmaker's bucket list as well. I think most filmmakers would rather be spending their time and effort making their next film, rather than exhaustively pushing their last in person and via aggressive emailing campaigns. Other than the (potential, anyhow) fiscal advantages of securing a traditional distribution deal, this is easily the biggest benefit to signing over the rights to your baby – not having to schlep it around the country on a college tour, tirelessly peddling DVDs to anyone and everyone willing to listen. My take on it falls right in line with those sentiments, but we still spent a solid year dabbling in self-distribution and publicity, unsure of whether traditional distribution was on the horizon. Because of all the post-production hiccups we experienced, particularly in the sound department, we actually began hitting up reviewers and such in late 2010, early 2011, thinking we'd have the film done much sooner than the actual June-ish completion date.

Once we did have a film we were comfortable urging others to watch, and some decent reviews started to roll in (most of which can be found listed in the external reviews section of the film's IMDb page, imdb.com/title/tt1261964/, because I took the time to submit them to the database – something you probably will have to do yourself also) we felt that we owed it to our investors to start taking steps towards monetization on our own, regardless of whether we would be able to find a distributor down the road. I designed a DVD case wraparound insert and disc label with my limited Adobe skills, and we printed off a limited 250-count run of DVDs through a local replicator (A to Z Media in New York) for around $600. These were sold via a PayPal link on the website, as well as in person at the festivals we played, and a few here and there out of the back of rental cars when one of us would head back home to visit friends and family. We eventually had to stop selling that version as part our distribution agreement - in the end, the last hundred or so of these were donated to a great charity that Ryan Gielen started, DVDs to the Troops (www.dvdstothetroops.org).

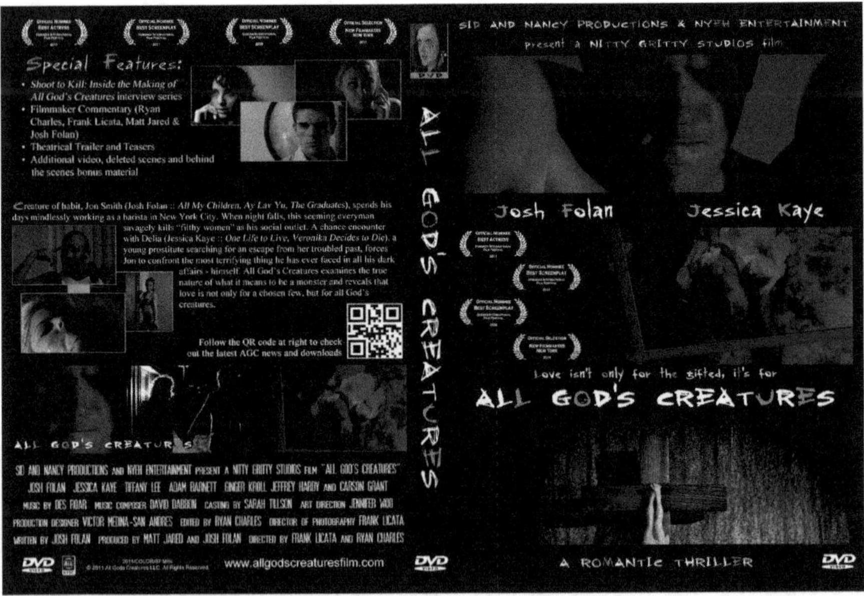

Limited-run AGC DVD wraparound

Finding a digital VOD platform was also something we felt we needed to do, and of all the options at the time we chose to go with IndieFlix (www.indieflix.com) for a number of reasons. They do not require an up-front encoding/processing fee, they do not require exclusivity, and their 70/30 revenue share was a reasonable one given the previous two advantages. Options here have ballooned since, but the most attractive platform I've seen of late is from a company I had brought to my attention at AFM last year called Screenburn (www.screenburn.com) that operates within a Facebook framework that I thought to be particularly sleek. Vimeo's filmmaker friendly reputation and generous 90/10 profit split also makes their platform quite attractive. This is an ever-evolving means of reaching your audience, and by the time I finish writing this paragraph there will likely be something bigger and better out there, so always google your ass off when deciding what direction to go with digital VOD at any given time.

There are some schools of thought that suggest your attractiveness to distributors is greater if your film has not been exposed to, and in turn pirated by, the interwebs at all. There were questions raised among the core group on AGC as to whether we would help or hinder our chances of getting a deal by selling the film ourselves. In hindsight, I'd recommend any filmmaker unsure of their distribution prospects just pull the trigger and start getting it out there. Long gone are the days of traditional distribution windows, when a theatrical release preceded the home DVD/video release, followed by a network television debut, then cable, so on and so forth. If anything, I'd think the fact we had dipped our toe in the marketplace infused some urgency into acquiring our film, as every sale we were potentially making was a lost one on a potential distributor's end. When we signed the deal we had to pull the DVD link off the website and take the film off of IndieFlix, but doing hardly constituted a backlash from self-distributing.

:: Indie Distribution Legal Checklist

:: Distribution. You'll first need to get together all those releases you responsibly amassed over this long, treacherous road. Those will need to be organized and given to a lawyer, who will check those and the final cut of the film itself to make a judgment as to whether he/she believes there are any risks that could come back to bite you in the ass later on. If there are none, the lawyer will write up a letter of opinion stating just that; if there are concerns, you will have to go back and address them. Once that letter is in hand, you can then deliver that to the errors and omissions insurer of your choice and fork over the exorbitant sum of cash required for the premium.

:: The distribution deal. Fight for what you think is right, don't settle because you're "just a no-name filmmaker."

:: Every self-distribution licensing agreement you enter into. If you are handling your own distribution, you should approach each deal with the same level of scrutiny you would approach a deal with a distribution company.

CUT TO:

THE END

In Closing (It's Never Really Over)

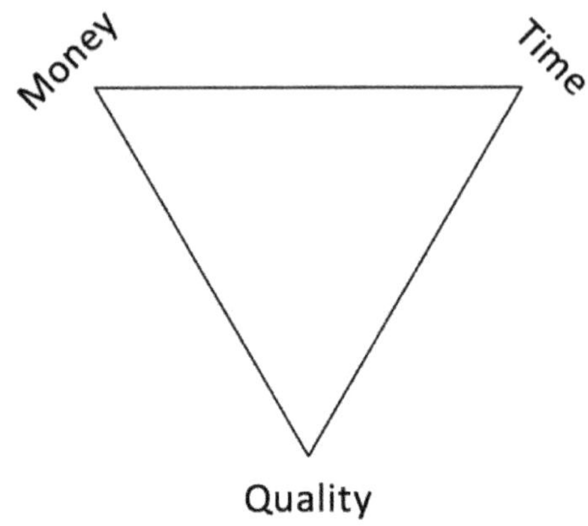

Money-Time-Quality Paradigm

That's how we did what we did, for better or worse. The only reason I left anything out, at least knowingly, was to respect the privacy of those who were kind enough to help us make this thing happen, so I hope the learning curve we experienced throughout the process will be of benefit to at least a few of my indie filmmaking brethren. I'm sure there's some things I have yet to be hit in the face with, even on a project that is approaching a year removed from its DVD street date, so my last lecture in this text is to understand the workload of producing a feature film for commercial purposes never really peters out – at least if you're a producer doing your investors the justice they deserve for believing in you. Your pursuit to monetize the film and drive revenue into the company that owns it should never fizzle out, regardless of how far removed from it your filmmaking career takes you. DiCaprio has a somewhat pretentious quote out there that goes "pain is temporary, film is forever," and that applies many times over for us micro-budget producers trying to squeeze a little blood from these turnips we put so much into creating. So go tend to your turnip patch, and do your best to help whenever you see a colleague having trouble with their own – a little more open collaboration and transparency would make this shit a lot easier for all of us.

FADE OUT.

Appendix L: Cynical Micro-Budget Filmmaking Glossary

:: **Advance:** The Holy Grail of the distribution deal, it is the sum of guaranteed money the distributor pays out to the filmmaker just for signing the paperwork. It's recoupable, meaning they deduct it back from sales before paying anything out to the filmmaker, but because of distributor accounting methodology and a few factors beyond their control, it can be the only money the filmmaker ever sees – hence the attractiveness of negotiating a deal inclusive of one.

:: **Breakdown Services:** The company that owns and operates the industry standard for putting out the casting breakdowns actors and (hopefully) their representatives will review and submit to while you are looking to fill out the cast on your project.

:: **B-Roll:** "Simple" shots that need to be captured for transitional images in a film – a train whizzing by, exterior establishing shots of a building, etc.

:: **Casting Breakdowns:** The cleverly-worded character descriptions that are sent out to prospective talent at the start of the casting process, ideally by your casting director and through Breakdown Services.

:: **Deliverables:** The seemingly impossible-to-procure list of masters, clearances and miscellaneous documents that a distributor requires from the filmmaker in order to fulfill a distribution agreement.

:: **Film Commissions:** Most large cities have offices subsidized by tax dollars that are in place to help attract film production to their respective areas. They offer a number of invaluable services – local crew hiring assistance, location scouting information, permit acquisition, to name a few.

:: **Finishing Funds:** The money a well-funded filmmaker has set aside in the budget for things like titles, sound mixing, ADR, etc. The micro-budget filmmaker obtains these through far more creative means – crowdfunding, begging relatives, selling plasma...things like that.

:: **Negotiating:** Begging.

:: **Picture Lock:** the numerous times through post-production where you will finalize the picture edit for the very last time. Ever. For sure this time. Really. I'm serious, dude.

:: **Preliminary Key Art:** the 27x39-inch signature branding image for the film that is used up through production, after which you will create a traditional key art image from production stills. It could be illustrated, stock photography, a hybrid of the two, or a better idea of your own – but it should essentially feel like a "movie poster."

:: **Production Bible:** a binder filled with every single piece of information that could possibly be needed to facilitate the execution of the film shoot. The script, elemental breakdowns of it, cast and crew contact sheet, location worksheets, shooting schedule, extra talent releases, etc.

:: **QC Reporting:** quality control reporting. A requisite in most all distribution agreements, it basically means hiring an independent editing facility to go through your film's master and measure a number of picture and sound elements to ensure they meet various broadcast and exhibition standards. It's a bit of a racket, seeing as a great deal of it is an opinion – meaning the company you hire and the company your distributor hires may very well have differing points of view on how the film measures up to those standards.

:: **Renegade:** a low-budget philosophy where you shoot quickly and off-the-cuff in places you can't afford to properly secure permission and/or permits to shoot in. You're not supposed to do this, because it's risky – but so is trying to make a movie for next to nothing in the first place.

:: **Shoot Out:** Finishing the shooting, as quickly as possible, of a production element – often an actor, but it can be a prop, vehicle, location or other costly element – because he/she/it is a stress-inducing suckhole on your miniscule production budget.

:: **Slate:** An actor stating their name for the camera before starting an audition for two reasons; One, so you have their name when reviewing the clips later, should you botch the media labeling. Two, so you can see them on camera being “themselves” for a moment before getting into character.

:: **Table Read:** a gathering of individuals vested in the project from which the latest draft of the script is read aloud, seemingly as poor as possible, for what I have decided is the sole purpose of inciting unease in those vested listeners.

:: **Withoutabox:** the film festival gate keeping monopoly that you submit to most festivals through. Some of the big guns (Tribeca and SXSW) have shunned the IMDb-owned entity, but most have embraced what is ultimately a fairly well-run service.

Appendix O: AGC Business Plan Outline

EXECUTIVE SUMMARY

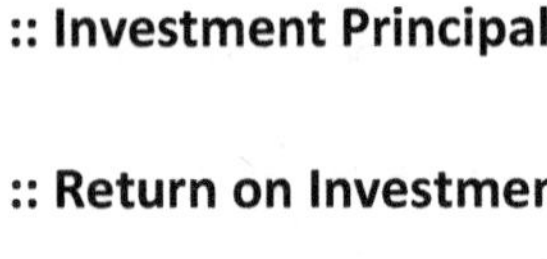

:: **Investment Principal**

:: **Return on Investment**

:: **Producers**

:: **Directors**

THE PRODUCTION

:: **Logline**

:: **Synopsis**

:: **Business Objectives**

:: **Screenplay Rights**

:: **Budget**

:: **Casting**

:: **Production Plan**

PRODUCER OVERVIEW

:: **Our Mission**

:: **Business Philosophy**

:: Investors' Recoupment

:: Risks

ADDENDUM

:: Motion Picture Production/Distribution Overview

Appendix V: Film 101 – Your Syllabus

In my perpetual sifting through the mostly useless piles of ones and zeroes that I've mainlined over the years I've been working in this industry, I'm willing to go to bat for the titles in the following list. I've categorized them because I have an organization fetish (the producer in me), and tacked on an aloof quote to each category because I find that literary practice amusing (the writer in me).

History :: "Those who don't know the mistakes of the past won't be able to enjoy it when they make them again in the future." – Diane Elizabeth Duane

:: *Easy Riders, Raging Bulls* by Peter Biskind – An intrusive look into the power shift from studio to auteur in 60's, 70's and 80's Hollywood from very simply the greatest film journalist of our time. Altman, Coppola, Spielberg, Scorsese, Nicholson, Beatty, Redford, etc.

:: *Down and Dirty Pictures* by Peter Biskind – Chronicles the rise of the Weinstein brothers and, more generally, the independent film movement of the 1980's.

:: *The Mailroom* by David Rensin – It's not just hearsay that some of Hollywood's biggest historical players started in mailrooms. Ovitz, Geffen, Diller and more.

:: *Star* by (you guessed it) Peter Biskind – Warren Beatty unplugged.

Memoirs :: "Besides, life is too short to spend it in the company of morons." – Jerry Weintraub

:: *When I Stop Talking, You'll Know I'm Dead* by Jerry Weintraub and Rich Cohen – No one embodies "making it happen" more so than Weintraub.

:: *Rebel Without A Crew* by Robert Rodriguez – Rodriguez explains the process of creating and selling his first feature, *El mariachi*.

:: *Tough Shit* by Kevin Smith – Indie royalty talks about the rise and fall of his love for the industry.

:: *So You Want to Be a Producer* by Lawrence Turman – Another legendary producer explains how he made it.

:: *She's Gotta Have It* by Spike Lee – How Spike got that all-important first feature done and out into the world.

Interview Compilations :: "Life's hard. But it's a lot harder if you're stupid." - Robert Mitchum

:: *Breaking In* by Nicholas Jarecki – Jarecki interviews twenty mainstream directors about the making of their first feature film.

:: *Screen Plays* by David S. Cohen – How twenty-five scripts made it down the long, hard road to getting produced.

:: *My First Movie: Take Two* by Stephen Lowenstein – Ten directors talk about getting it done for the first time.

Industry Analysis :: "Most films are bad. They are, finally, just advertisements for themselves - elongated movie trailers, envisioned and cut with less skill than the trailer itself." - David Mamet

:: *Bambi vs. Godzilla* by David Mamet – A cynical look at Hollywood through the eyes of a guy who doesn't give a shit about the rules.

Screenwriting :: "You sell a screenplay like you sell a car. If someone drives it off a cliff, that's it." – Rita Mae Brown

:: *Save the Cat* by Blake Snyder – The screenwriting bible when it comes to structure. If you haven't read it yet, delete Celtx and Final Draft from your computer immediately.

:: *Alternative Scriptwriting* by Ken Dancyger – After you've read Save the Cat, learn how to safely break all those rules you should never break.

Producing :: "A producer is a man with a dream. I say, 'I don't write, I don't direct, I don't act, I don't compose music, I don't design costumes. What do I do? I make things happen.'" - David Wolper

:: *Independent Feature Film Production* by Gregory Goodell – An in-depth analysis of every step on the road to completing and releasing a feature film.

:: *Bankroll* by Tom Malloy – Malloy talks the mentality behind finding financing as an independent producer.

:: *Filmmakers & Financing* by Louise Levinson – The focus is on budgeting, but Levinson delves out a ton of useful advice here.

:: *Dealmaking in the Film & Television Industry* by Mark Litwak – A veteran entertainment attorney's compendium of film contracts, specifically targeted for the low-budget realm.

:: *The Movie Business* by Kelly Charles Crabb – Another seasoned entertainment attorney delves into the nuts and bolts of entertainment law.

Low-Budget Filmmaking :: "And that's what so much of making movies is about: fighting." - Sidney Lumet

:: *Feature Filmmaking at Used-Car Prices* by Rick Schmidt – Ideas galore for getting a film done without having the actual money required to do so.

:: *Fast, Cheap, and Under Control* by John Gaspard – The story of thirty-three indies that you've actually seen, which means they were successful. Lots to learn from this.

Marketing & Distribution :: "To you guys from the coasts, the country is New York and LA. Everything in between is just the blur you fly over. But I'll tell you, the blur is where the audience lives and where you make your money." - Colonel Tom Parker

:: *Think Outside the Box Office* by Jon Reiss – An uber-contemporary look at marketing your film in today's DIY, digitaly-minded marketplace.

:: *The Business of Media Distribution* by Jeff Ulin – This is actually a boring-as-hell read, but if you don't know everything about the distribution process, you will after reading it.

If you've read a title worth my time that's not on this list, by all means shoot me an enlightening email at filmmakingthehardway@nyehentertainment.com.

Appendix E: All God's Creatures Script

Download the full All God's Creatures shooting script at

nyehentertainment.com/downloads/agcscript.pdf.

The Author

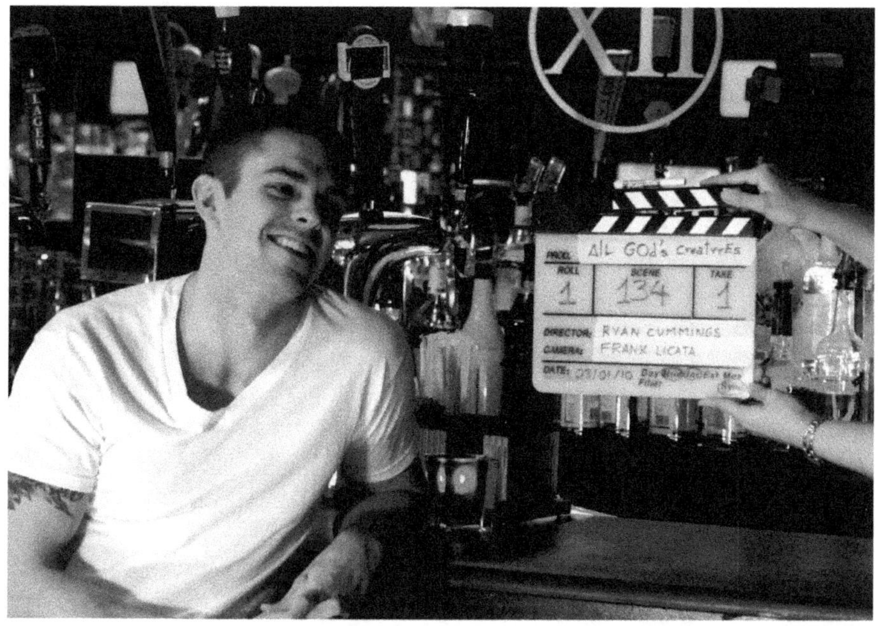

Folan on set of All God's Creatures

Josh Folan is a producer, writer, director and actor with professional credits dating back to 2005. His first feature-length film venture, the romantic thriller *All God's Creatures*, was released through Osiris Entertainment in May of 2012 and can be purchased through the film's website at www.allgodscreaturesfilm.com. Folan wrote, produced and starred in the film, which premiered at the 2011 Hoboken International Film Festival where it was nominated for best screenplay and best actress (Jessica Kaye). His second feature, a slacker buddy comedy titled *What Would Bear Do?*, is available at www.whatwouldbeardofilm.com. Folan wrote, produced and starred in it as well, in addition to taking on directorial duties for the first time. *Filmmaking, the Hard* Way is his first crack at writing a book, and you can follow him (@joshfolan) and his production company, NYEH

Entertainment (@nyehentertains :: www.nyehentertainment.com), on twitter and facebook if you'd like to keep up with his shit.

www.ingramcontent.com/pod-product-compliance
Lightning Source LLC
LaVergne TN
LVHW010618100826
845148LV00014B/3026
9780615822358